Ghostly Sights

St. Bonaventure presenting a text for meditation, MS Royal 20, BNP3, by permission of the British Library.

GHOSTLY SIGHTS

Visual Meditation
in
Late-Medieval Literature

by
Denise Despres

PILGRIM BOOKS
NORMAN, OKLAHOMA

Library of Congress Cataloging-in-Publication Data

Despres, Denise Louise, 1958–
   Ghostly sights: visual meditation in late-medieval literature /
by Denise Despres. — 1st ed.
     p. cm.
   Includes bibliographical references.
   ISBN 0-937664-81-2 : $29.95
   1. English literature — Middle English, 1100–1500 — History and
criticism.   2. Christian literature, English (Middle) — History and
criticism.   3. Franciscans — England — History.   4. Meditation in
literature.   5. Visions in literature.   I. Title.
PR275.R4D47   1989
820.9'382'0902 — dc20   89-38444
                                                       CIP

Published by Pilgrim Books
P.O. Box 2399, Norman, Oklahoma 73070
Copyright © 1989 by Pilgrim Books
Manufactured in the U.S.A.   First edition.   All rights reserved.

For Stephen

Contents

List of Illustrations

Preface

No faculty is more essential to a sacramental religion than the imagination. The intangible mysteries of the Trinity, of the Resurrection, or of transubstantiation elicit visual responses from all neophytes, whether they are adults probing a new theology or children memorizing their catechism. As medieval theologians from Augustine to Bonaventure were quick to point out, sight is our primary means of cognition, and the imagination is thus central to the process of conversion. The term "imagination," however, has come only very recently to its current meaning. What then does Margery Kempe's amanuensis mean when he says that Margery "ymagyned" or envisioned her own martyrdom soon after her conversion? And why does she call this grisly beheading scene to memory, before her inward eye, for careful scrutiny? Such visionary activity is central to Margery Kempe's spiritual awakening, yet religious and literary scholars have only begun to explore its influence on her own spiritual expression and its formative role in the development of Western spirituality.

Late-medieval lyrics, spiritual autobiographies, hagiographies, and dream visions are full of such "ghostly sights." Without an understanding of their function and importance in late-medieval spiritual expression, we cannot comprehend fully the purpose of this literature or the complex bonds between what we might initially perceive as vastly different genres. Furthermore, we cannot account for literary phenomena like the profusion of visionary narratives, whether mystical, autobiographical, or fictional, in late-medieval England. Scholars have wondered why this literary activity occurred when it did in a religious climate marked for its conservatism, particularly when it is compared to the effusive, affective religious character of Continental piety.

This book explores the influence of Franciscan spirituality on visionary, or meditative, narratives in fourteenth-century England. Certainly meditation, which exercises the visual imagination, did not originate with the Franciscans. No other religious order, however, played so central a role in the shaping of lay piety or gained the popularity of the friars in the century after they accepted their vocation as evangelists, preachers, and teachers. As confessors, penitential advisers, and instructors they had the greatest impact on the dissemination of sermon collections, penitential manuals, and gospel harmonies of any religious order. Although my discussion focuses on the impact of *Meditations on the Life of Christ*, the most popular late-medieval gospel harmony, I hope to call attention to this remarkable and neglected body of instructional materials.

Scholars have recently pointed out the difficulties in ascribing the influence of any one religious order on medieval literary production. Michael Sargent, for example, argues that "the composition and transmission of such literature must depend upon the evidence of the manuscripts in which the literature survives, and not merely upon its perceived compatibility with the spirituality of the order."[1] Without overlooking the vital importance of manuscript studies, I hope to convince my readers that we can distinguish the unique elements of Franciscan spirituality in works of Franciscan origins and reconstruct their effect on English religious narrative. Nicholas Love, a Carthusian, did indeed translate *Meditations on the Life of Christ*. This does not alter the Franciscan nature of the gospel harmony; rather, it reinforces our knowledge of the appeal that Franciscan theology, based on visionary experience and the apostolic ideal, held for medieval penitents.

[1] Michael G. Sargent, "Bonaventura English: A Summary of the Middle English Prose Translations of Early Franciscan Literature," *ACar* 106, no. 2 (1987): 147.

Other scholars, such as Penn R. Szittya, have convinced us that the antifraternal literary tradition in England manifested itself after 1360, a full century after it reached its fullest expression in France. The same appears to be true of Franciscan literary expression, with the exception of the lyric. At the very time that lay penitents appear to have been hungering for Franciscan meditative texts, personalizing the path of *imitatio*, poets like Langland and Chaucer were challenging the Franciscan ideal. I hope that this preliminary investigation of Franciscan narrative may contribute something to future research in this area.

There are several studies whose importance I wish to acknowledge, although they were published after the completion of my own. Chief among these are Penn R. Szittya's *The Antifraternal Tradition in Medieval Literature* (1986), necessary reading for students of Franciscan literary tradition; Caroline W. Bynum's *Holy Feast and Holy Fast* (1987); and Elizabeth Petroff's *Medieval Women's Visionary Literature* (1986). The last two works have profoundly changed the way we think about medieval women's spirituality. Scholarship on Margery Kempe has blossomed in the past few years, and I direct my readers to articles by Valerie Lagorio, David Wallace, Sue Ellen Holbrook, and Karma Lochrie, easily found in recent MLA bibliographies and in bibliographies dealing with the mystics.

DENISE DESPRES
The University of Puget Sound
Tacoma, Washington

Acknowledgments

I am deeply grateful to the Charlotte W. Newcombe Foundation of Princeton University and to the Graduate School of Indiana University, both of which provided me with generous financial support while I researched and wrote this book. Their assistance gave me the time and leisure to follow various intellectual paths unhampered by the usual constraints of academic life. In addition, The University of Puget Sound facilitated revisions by awarding me a Martin Nelson Summer Research Fellowship and a Martin Nelson Junior Sabbatical. Selections from the original text have appeared in *Mystics Quarterly*, *Franciscan Studies*, and *The Downside Review*.

I am indebted also to Alfred David, Judith Anderson, and Eugene Kintgen for their patience and kindness. Other mentors who have contributed to the long-term success of this project are Valerie Lagorio, who has paved the way for students of the female mystics; and Dolores Warwick Frese, who introduced me to medieval literature many years ago. To Lawrence Clopper I can only return simple thanks with affection. His sound intellectual advice and rigorous expectations have taught me a great deal about scholarship; his good cheer, encouragement, and modesty, about maintaining equilibrium.

I would like to thank my parents, whose guidance and optimism have been an invaluable source of energy. This book is dedicated to my husband, Stephen. His generous sacrifices, small and large, for my achievement are too numerous to count.

D.L.D.

Ghostly Sights

And þerfor þe sayd creatur must nedys wepyn & cryin whan sche sey swech gostly syȝtys in hir sowle as freschly & as verily as ȝyf it had ben don in dede in hir bodily syght... (*The Book of Margery Kempe*, p. 190, lines 26–29)

The Crucifixion, MS Digby 227, fol. 113ᵛ, by permission of the Bodleian Library, Oxford University.

1

Introduction

Franciscan spirituality is most often associated with the emphasis in late-medieval piety on the pathetic elements of Christ's humanity. Although some of the most eloquent personal expressions of this kind of devotion are to be found in the affective writings of Bernard and Anselm, the Franciscans touched a common chord of sympathy through popular verbal and pictorial images of the Virgin and Child and the degradation of the Crucifixion. The Franciscan penitential lyrics of the thirteenth and fourteenth centuries show how the imaginative re-creation of the Crucifixion scene in particular provided the dramatic setting for meditation, or for the vicarious experience of Christ's love and suffering that was essential in fulfilling the Franciscan desire for complete identification with Christ.[1]

The purpose of affective devotion, as developed by Bonaventure in Franciscan theology and implemented by the Preaching Friars in penitential programs, was to arouse feelings of remorse in the penitent that would move the will to contrition. While the term "affective" suggests that the function of this imaginative, participatory devotion was entirely emotive, a brief examination of a penitential lyric from an early

[1] Rosemary Woolf, *An Introduction to the Religious Lyric in the Middle Ages*, p. 44. See pp. 21–33 for a discussion of the theology of affective devotion.

Franciscan manuscript (British Museum MS Royal 12E) reveals its purpose of providing the occasion for self-examination and resolution:

> Whanne ic se on Rode
> Jesu, my lemman
> And besiden him stonden
> Marye and Johan,
> And his rig iswongen,
> And his side istungen,
> For the luve of man;
> Well ou ic to wepen,
> And sinnes for to leten,
> Yif ic of luve can,
> Yif ic of luve can,
> Yif ic of luve can.[2]

When reading this lyric, one cannot help thinking of Erich Auerbach's penetrating comparison of Francis's own breathless, natural prose, immediate in its utter simplicity, with Bernard's learned and elegant rhetoric.[3] Like Francis's own writing — the little we have of it — the lyric is experiential; its power of expression lies in its appeal to the reader to follow its visual movement — a sweeping survey of the cross that ultimately focuses on the bitter reality of the Crucifixion: the wound in Christ's side that became a compelling image in late-medieval devotional and mystical prose.

Although simple, the lyric's form relies on an established meditational scheme that all Franciscan meditation ultimately shared. Elizabeth Salter describes the three principal stages of Christocentric meditation as (1) sensible recollection, (2) emotional reflection, and (3) moral application.[4] Briefly, sensible recollection provides the focus for the meditation by vividly creating a scene of a gospel event in the imagination. Emotional reflection is the meditator's nondiscursive or initial response to the scene: the willful soul, confronted with Christ's mercy and compassion, becomes aware of its own sinful nature that prevents the return of this love. Self-awareness naturally leads to moral

---

[2] R. T. Davies, ed., *Medieval English Lyrics*, p. 99.
[3] Erich Auerbach, *Mimesis*, p. 166. Also see pp. 167–73 on the influence of Franciscanism on medieval culture.
[4] Elizabeth Salter, *Nicholas Love's* Myrrour of the Blessed Lyf of Jesu Christ, vol. 10 of *Analecta Cartusiana*, ed. James Hogg, p. 158.

application, or a resolution to reform. The typical meditation ends with a plea for guidance, a colloquy, or an expression of love.[5]

The first six lines of the lyric above are an imaginative re-creation of a traditionally iconographic scene familiar to us from medieval art and drama. The meditation in lines 7 and 8, however, shifts the attention back to the observer and his or her own sinful life. Finally, the focus returns to the sacrifice that is beyond earthly understanding: the last three lines express a painfully human inability to comprehend the mystery of the Passion, defined in terms of "luve" beyond human experience. Franciscan meditation on Christ's humanity enabled the penitent, educated or uneducated, male or female, to experience the Passion personally and to scrutinize his or her individual response.

The virtues of such meditation are primarily moral, explains the Franciscan author of *Meditations on the Life of Christ*, a thirteenth-century gospel harmony that teaches a Poor Clare the spiritual benefits of envisioning Christ's life:

> But you must know that it is not necessary for the active life to precede this contemplation, for it contains corporal matters, that is the works of Christ according to humanity, as is proposed more easily, not to the most perfect, but to the vulgar, to look at, for in it, as in the active, we purge ourselves of vices and fill ourselves with virtues, and thus this converges with the active.[6]

For the Franciscans, who led a "mixed" life of service and contemplation, meditations on Christ's humanity that provided moral illumination and elicited compassion were the best ways to teach the unlearned or the laity to prepare for penance. These spiritual exercises did not

---

[5] Ibid., p. 144.

[6] *Meditations on the Life of Christ*, trans. and ed. Isa Ragusa and Rosalie B. Green, p. 265. Subsequent translations are taken from this edition. All Latin passages from the *Meditationes* are provided in the footnotes and are cited from the following edition by chapter and page number (paragraphs are not numbered in this edition): *Meditationes vitae Christi*, in *Opera omnia Bonaventurae*, ed. A. C. Peltier, 12:509–630. See chap. 51, p. 577. The Latin reads: "Scire tamen debes, quod hanc contemplationem non oportet quod praecedet vita activa, quia de rebus corporalibus est, scilicet de actionibus Christi secundum humanitatem, Unde tanquam familiarior non tantum perfectioribus, sed etiam rudibus proponitur intuenda; tum quia in ea, sicut in activa, et a vitiis purgamur, et virtutibus imbuimur; unde haec cum activa concurrit." For an introduction to this important medieval meditative work and its spurious ascription to Bonaventure, see John Moorman, *A History of the Franciscan Order*, pp. 261–62.

aspire to contemplation or mystical revelation. Even the simplest medieval layperson knew enough of the gospel narrative to reconstruct important events from Christ's life. The Franciscans encouraged the laity to meditate freely on the Gospels and to use their imaginations. They instructed penitents to mesh individual history with the sacred history of Scripture, for only by experiencing life with Christ could the sinful fully understand the sympathy Christ had for the human condition and the nature of the supreme sacrifice he willingly chose through love. The penitent, in response to this gift, freely surrendered his or her own will in preparation for penance.

The emphasis throughout this kind of devotion is on experience, and that is not surprising. The Franciscan spiritual "world view" does not separate the tangible from the spiritual but is a conscious blend of experience and the authority of Scripture. Francis himself literally relied on the Gospels to direct his movement in the world: "Then Francis, who was devoted to the Trinity, opened the book of the Gospels three times. . . . The book opened the first time to the text: 'If you will be perfect, go, sell all that you have, and give to the poor.'"[7]

In turn, Francis's literal interpretation of the scriptural message enabled him to internalize the meaning of the Gospels through experience. This emphasis on experience is at the heart of the visionary trend in late-medieval England, popularized through a form of meditation that emphasized fellowship with Christ and a new concept of individual participation.

By the fifteenth century visual meditation was thoroughly integrated into private devotions, as the extensive manuscript tradition of works like the *Myrrour of the Blessed Lyf of Jesu Christ*, by Nicholas

[7] Bonaventure, *The Life of Francis*, in Bonaventure, *Works*, trans. and ed. Ewert Cousins, p. 201. The translations I have used from Bonaventure's *Life of St. Francis*, *Tree of Life*, and *The Soul's Journey into God* can be found in Bonaventure, *Works*, trans. and ed. Ewert Cousins; and Bonaventure, *Legenda S. Francisi* (*Legenda maior*), in *Opera omnia S. Bonaventurae* (Quaracchi, 1898), 8:504–64; see chap. 3, par. 3, p. 510. All Latin passages from the *Legenda maior* are cited from the latter edition by chapter, paragraph, and page number. The Latin reads: "Trinitatis Franciscus ter Evangeliorum librum aperuit, trino exposcens a Deo. . . . In prima libri apertione illud occurrit: 'Si vis perfectus esse, vade, vende omnia, quae habes, et da pauperibus.'" Also see this edition for the *Lignum vitae*, 8:68–87; and the *Itinerarium mentis in Deum*, 5:293–316.

Love, indicates.[8] Even before the rise of literacy in England, however, gospel harmonies, or scriptural paraphrases in the vernacular, like the *Meditations on the Supper of Our Lord* (1338) were read aloud to "congregacyons."[9] When they were listening to the Gospels, individuals were encouraged to imagine or re-create those scriptural scenes in detail to experience salvation history in an omnitemporal present. As we shall see in chapter 2, this kind of meditation is consistent with distinctive elements of Franciscan spirituality: it is penitential and participatory, and, most important, it requires the individual to assume responsibility in some capacity for the welfare of his or her own soul. As Susan Dickman states of Margery Kempe's spirituality, so heavily influenced by Franciscanism:

> It is in Kempe's individual and brilliant adaptation of what was originally a discipline for cloistered contemplatives that we see most clearly the interrelated questions which surround the transfer of religious authority from the institution to the private individual in late Medieval England.[10]

From the beginning, however, this religious freedom was an integral part of the Franciscan attitude toward prayer, meditation, and the balance of the active and contemplative lives. Francis's own perplexity about the merging of what monasticism considered two ways of serving God, unequal in merit, is reflected in what might be considered a dangerous absence of direction concerning prayer life from his revised Rule of 1223, the *Regula bullata*. Ultimately Francis's silence shaped the autonomous role of the Franciscan:

> The very nature of the mixed life of the Franciscan . . . carries with it a definite problem that has to be solved in a personal way that calls for more personal responsibility. That is why the *Regula Bullata* contains no legislation on prayer and is content to state the ideal.[11]

[8] Margaret Deanesly, "Vernacular Books in England in the Fourteenth and Fifteenth Centuries," *MLR* 15 (1920): 353.

[9] Margaret Deanesly, "The Gospel Harmony of John de Caulibus, or St. Bonaventura," in C. L. Kingsford, ed., *Collectanea Franciscana*, 2:19.

[10] Susan Dickman, "Margery Kempe and the English Devotional Tradition," in Marion Glasscoe, ed., *The Medieval Mystical Tradition in England*, Papers Read at the Exeter Symposium, July, 1980, p. 168.

[11] Ignatius Brady, "The History of Mental Prayer in the Order of Friars Minor," *FS* 11 (1951): 321. Brady explains that Francis tried to set the proper attitude toward prayer "by example," rather than by legislation, which resulted in "a problem that had not

Ignatius Brady points out that in giving his friars such freedom, "St. Francis has transferred to his Friars the ideal of mediaeval knighthood."[12] The cornerstone of mendicancy was a simple faith in God's daily provision for mankind that precluded a rigid adherence to any religious hierarchy or custom. Like the knights of the medieval romances, the early friars ventured out into the world to perform acts of charity. Through an active and spontaneous life of imitation they sought spiritual perfection. Francis himself adopted this *topos* of religious chivalry, giving it a radically new significance in the verbal iconography of lay spirituality. In *Mimesis*, Auerbach describes knighthood as a "personal and absolute ideal" and the knight's adventures as a "fated and gradual test of election: it becomes the basis of a doctrine of personal perfection."[13]

Whereas monasticism identified with this aristocratic, hierarchical conception of spirituality, Francis focused on the paradox of the Incarnation. Christ crucified was King of the Jews and all creation, but he chose to disguise his divinity under the cloak of simplicity and poverty. His true nobility was unveiled when, through courtesy and gentility, he bestowed his life for humankind's salvation. The purpose of the Franciscan evangelical movement was to transform this ideal, through penance and a heightening of religious sensibilities, from a vocation possible only for contemplatives to a life of charity possible for all Christians in differing degrees. If we examine early Franciscan biography, which is exemplary fiction, we see that the early apostles Rufino, Angelo, and Anthony of Padua are independent characters like Francis, who willingly accept rigorous penances and physical and spiritual challenges.

Nonetheless, this personal freedom was also a source of dissension after Francis's death, for only his most saintly followers were capable of emulating his poverty, humility, and childlike fervor, which was indeed the "ideal." The painful and violent dispute between the Spiritualists and the Conventualists challenged the possibility of the order's sur-

---

been posited for earlier religious life, for the monk in the seclusion of the abbey . . . the Friar Minor . . . was to be an apostle of action and yet a man of deep prayer; he had to maintain a balance of these elements" (p. 319).

[12] Ibid., p. 321.

[13] Auerbach, *Mimesis*, pp. 134, 136.

vival, and the hierarchical or feudal structure of the medieval church could not sustain an order founded on what was essentially a revolutionary concept of spiritual democracy, regardless of Francis's chivalric description of his Minorites.

Still, it is this element of individuality, firmly embedded in the order's structure, that made the Franciscans the most suitable choice for teaching penance to the laity and enabled the friars to cross cultural and geographical boundaries in medieval Europe. The Fourth Lateran Council's provisions for instituting penance caused radical changes in the lay individual's perception of his or her role in salvation history that were consistent with spiritual developments in Francis's own life. Like that of any other sinner's, Francis's spiritual life began with conversion; and unlike the Latin saints' lives in the *Legenda aurea* — tales of rational defiance, cool rejection of earthly passion, and certain martyrdom — Francis's life is depicted as a constant struggle with sensuality, anger, and pride and a slow realization of his perfect sanctity.

In 1260, Francis's dedicated follower Bonaventure was chosen at the General Chapter of Narbonne to write a biography of the saint. His *Life of Francis*, or *Legenda maior*, has been the frequent subject of discussion among scholars of Franciscanism like Rosalinde Brooke and John Moorman, who rightly speculate about its political aims. Ultimately the biography portrays a more tempered view of Francis's spirituality than the zealous "primitive spirit" sketched in earlier lives of the saint.[14] Nevertheless, Bonaventure's threefold way of purgation, illumination, and perfection established an inward pattern of conformity to Christ initiated with penance — a Franciscan path of *imitatio* that appealed to the laity:

> Set on fire by the fervour of his preaching, a great number of people bound themselves by new laws of penance according to the rule which they received from the man of God. Christ's servant decided to name this way of life the Order of the Brothers of Penance. As the road of Penance is common to all who are striving

[14] Bonaventure, *Works*, trans. and ed. Cousins, introduction, p. 41. See also Moorman, *A History of the Franciscan Order*, pp. 151–52, 286–87. Moorman notes that, as minister general, Bonaventure "had two objects in mind — to justify the Order in the eyes of the world and to draw the conflicting parties among the friars into greater concord. When we look at the *Legenda* we see how closely it fits this double policy" (p. 287).

toward heaven, so this way of life admits clerics and laity, single and married of both sexes.[15]

In the *Legenda maior*, Bonaventure depicts Francis in a prophetic role, which suits the biographer's purpose of defining Francis's vocation, and hence the order's mission: "Like John the Baptist, he was appointed by God to prepare in the desert a way of the highest poverty and to preach repentance by word and example."[16] In his own *Final Testament*, however, Francis describes his life and vocation simply in terms of penance and remission in a highly personal manner: "The Lord granted me, brother Francis, to begin to do penance in this way, that when I was in sin it seemed to me very terrible to see lepers, and the Lord led me among them, and I helped them."[17]

Francis, the merchant's son, conceived his conversion in the tradition of Paul, the bourgeois tax collector, whose spiritual blindness became a physical blindness until Christ restored his vision of a moral order. Francis's typically medieval dread of the diseased, viewed as tainted and sinful outcasts much like the early Christians whom Paul persecuted, was a sign of his own sinfulness and spiritual limitations. Only Christ could personally lead him among the sick without fear, to reestablish charity. To Francis, however, remission meant that each individual must personally conform "inwardly and outwardly" to Christ.[18] It was not enough to submit the individual will without manifesting this change through action. Francis taught his disciples that penance requires rigorous self-examination and consequently a constant reevaluation of

[15] Bonaventure, *Life of St. Francis*, in *Works*, trans. and ed. Cousins, p. 210. The Latin reads: "Nam praedicationis ipsius fervore succensi, quam plurimi secundum formam a Dei viro acceptam novis se poenitentiae legibus vinciebant, quorum vivendi modum idem Christi famulus Ordinem Fratrum de poenitentia nominari decrevit. Nimirum sicut in caelum tendentibus poenitentiae viam omnibus constat esse communem, sic et hic status clericos et laicos, virgines et coniugatos in utroque sexu admittens, quanti sit apud Deum meriti, ex pluribus per aliquos ipsorum patratis miraculis innotescit." Bonaventure, *Legenda*, chap. 4, par. 6, p. 514.

[16] Bonaventure, *Life of Francis*, in *Works*, trans. and ed. Cousins, p. 180. The Latin reads: "Secundum imitatoriam quoque similitudinem praecursoris destinatus a Deo, ut, viam parans in deserto altissimae paupertatis, tam exemplo quam verbo poenitentiam praedicaret." Bonaventure, *Legenda*, prol., par. 1, p. 504.

[17] Francis, *Testament*, in Rosalinde B. Brooke, trans. and ed., *The Coming of the Friars*, p. 117.

[18] Ibid., p. 119.

personal history. He expressed his own conversion in the characteristically dramatic act of renouncing his past life, as the son of the mercenary Pietro Bernadone, before the bishop of Assisi; he literally stripped off his "old clothes," as Paul demanded, to become a "new man" in Christ (Eph. 4:22–25). Bonaventure's depiction of this symbolic scene was faithfully translated into English as early as 1291 in the *Early South English Legendary*:

> He seide, "ich þe habbe fader i-cleoped: evere to þis day,
> And nouþe it is so feor i-come þat non more i ne may,
> Segge ich mot mi pater-noster; heonne-forth þe word i-wis
> And to mi fader holde me: þat in hevene is.[19]

After his conversion Francis created a personal rule that required unearthly strength and courage. Like Christ, he embraced poverty and ministered primarily to his society's outcasts. Unlike Cistercian or Bernardine devotion, therefore, which is rooted in an intellectual, monastic tradition, Franciscan spirituality, as manifested in the *Regula bullata*, is Francis's personal spirituality. Franciscan spirituality in the biographies of Celano or Saint Bonaventure, and even in Franciscan theological works like the *Itinerarium mentis in Deum*, is largely the writer's experiential response to Francis's unique and inspiring spirituality.

For example, Bonaventure's own literal and mystical ascent on Mount Alverna provided the occasion for the *Itinerarium* (1259), which placed Franciscan devotion in a theological framework; nonetheless, the work is initially Bonaventure's private search for an inner peace like Francis's—one that would enable him to complete the formidable task of regularizing the Order, a task that discouraged Francis himself:

> Following the example of our most blessed Father Francis, I was seeking this peace with panting spirit—I a sinner and utterly unworthy, who after our blessed Father's death had become the seventh Minister General of the Friars. It happened that about the time of the thirty-third anniversary of the Saint's death, under divine impulse, I withdrew to the Mount La Verna, seeking a place of quiet and desiring to find there peace of spirit. While I was there reflecting on various ways by which the soul ascends into God, there came to mind, among other things, the miracle which had occurred to blessed Francis in this very place: the vision of a winged seraph in

[19] Carl Horstmann, ed., *The Early South English Legendary*, 87:56.

the form of the Crucified. While reflecting on this, I saw at once that this vision represented our father's rapture in contemplation and the road by which this rapture is reached.[20]

John Fleming states that the "Franciscan life is a life of double movement, of an outward journey and an inward one."[21] Both Francis and Bonaventure ascended Mount Alverna, in the Umbrian Apennines, literally and figuratively climbing the spiritual ladder to perfection that becomes the mystical motif for spiritual growth in religious works throughout the Middle Ages. Fleming's statement probes the very mystery and attraction of Franciscan spirituality, however, with its emphasis on the incarnational element of Christianity. Spiritual biography, or the selective narrative of a life manifesting spiritual change through action or symbol, was the natural response to those early followers of Francis who were trying to comprehend his existence. Acknowledging Francis's path of *imitatio*, his biographers openly suggest a schematic correlation between the saint's life and Christ's by directly recalling scenes from the Gospels and narrating events of his lifelike parables. Like Franciscan meditation, therefore, which makes events in the Gospels alive for the individual, Franciscan exemplary fiction permeates "sacred time," or the mythical time of Christ's life reattained through liturgical ritual, by placing the lives of the saint and his followers in a scriptural context.[22]

Similarly, in the course of the arduous spiritual, physical, and

[20] Bonaventure, *The Soul's Journey into God*, in Bonaventure, *Works*, trans. and ed. Cousins, p. 54. The Latin reads: "Cum igitur exemplo beatissimi patris Francisci hanc pacem anhelo spiritu quaererem, ego peccator, qui loco ipsius patris beatissimi post eius transitum septimus in generali fratrum ministerio per omnia indignus succedo; contigit, ut nutu divino circa Beati ipsius transitum, anno trigesimo tertio ad montem Alvernae tanquam ad locum quietum amore quaerendi pacem spiritus declinarem, ibique existens, dum mente tractarem aliquas mentales ascensiones in Deum, inter alia occurit illud miraculum, quod in praedicto loco contigit ipsi beato Francisco, de visione scilicet Seraph alati ad instar Crucifixi. In cuius consideratione statim visum est mihi, quod visio illa praetenderet ipsius patris suspensionem in contemplando et viam, per quam pervenitur ad eam." Bonaventure, *Itinerarium in mentis Deum*, prologue, par. 2, p. 295.

[21] John Fleming, *An Introduction to the Franciscan Literature of the Middle Ages*, p. 8.

[22] Mircea Eliade, *Patterns in Comparative Religion*, p. 388. See chap. 11, "Sacred Time and the Myth of the Eternal Return," pp. 388–409, for an excellent exposition of sacramentalism and incarnational spirituality.

14

psychological pilgrimages in *The Book of Margery Kempe*, *Pearl* and *Piers Plowman*, individual experience blends with scriptural scenes in dreamlike or meditative states, dissolving the boundaries of time and space. The penitents, all willful, hungry souls, observe or participate in these scenes. Each narrator is converted by a revelation of God's love, humbled, and made contrite. At these points in the works—Margery Kempe's *Book*, *Pearl* and *Piers Plowman*—the life of the narrator is placed in the context of salvation history. The present "only acquires its meaning in relation to that history."[23]

As David Jeffrey notes:

> Where traditional medieval exegesis involved the concordance of the two Testaments, a concordance of symbols, of spiritual truths, Franciscan exegetes extended the concordance to current events and ultimately to personal history. The point of interpretation and its appropriate conclusion was participation.[24]

Recent studies of late-medieval lay piety and affective devotion have increasingly tended to examine Franciscan spirituality in works that we have traditionally admitted into the secularized canon of English literature. Jeffrey's *Early English Lyric and Franciscan Spirituality* suggests that further study in this area will yield an equally rich understanding of works that we seldom associate with penitential literature. "Penitential literature" usually refers to the predominantly mendicant teaching manuals and courtesy books that helped the clergy integrate the sacrament of penance into Roman Catholic lay life. "Conversion" poems like *Pearl* and *Piers Plowman*, which dramatize the conformity of the will to God's, as well as spiritual autobiographies like Margery Kempe's *Book*, indicate the extent to which the Franciscans shaped the popular religious imagination.

While educating the laity in the fundamental doctrines of the Catholic religion, the Franciscans simultaneously provided patterns of experience, or "metaphors," to order individual spiritual development.[25] Franciscan spirituality thus manifested itself in a tradition of

---

[23] Mary J. Carruthers, "Time, Apocalypse, and the Plot of *Piers Plowman*," in Mary J. Carruthers and Elizabeth D. Kirk, eds., *Acts of Interpretation: The Text in Its Contexts, 700–1600: Essays on Medieval and Renaissance Literature in Honor of E. Talbot Donaldson*, p. 184.

[24] David Jeffrey, *The Early English Lyric and Franciscan Spirituality*, p. 47.

[25] James Olney, *Metaphors of Self*, p. 47.

15

"experiential" literature in England: in the meditative gospel harmonies that encourage imaginative participation, in Franciscan biography that re-creates Scripture to celebrate individual conversion and imitation of Christ, and, finally, in three of the most significant examples of lay spirituality in late-medieval English literature. Franciscan devotion enabled the laity to merge personal history with salvation history through an established meditative tradition, in a manner previously limited to those who led monastic lives.

Chapter 2 of this book, therefore, explores visual meditation and creates a historical and literary context for reading such widely disseminated gospel harmonies as *Meditations on the Life of Christ* and *Meditations on the Supper of Our Lord*. Chapter 3 illustrates how visual meditation and the Franciscan gospel harmonies provided Margery Kempe, a fifteenth-century English laywoman, with the narrative structure upon which to pattern her own spiritual experiences. Margery's *Book* depicts her inner and outer conformity to Christ and is thus a spiritual autobiography. Of equal importance, Margery's *Book* suggests that Franciscan participatory meditation, which requires the penitent to envision imaginatively or re-create scriptural events, is directly related to other creative acts, such as narrating personal history, parables, or tales, as Margery does in the course of her story.

In chapters 4 and 5, I discuss two dream poems that illustrate the psychological process of conversion, *Pearl* and *Piers Plowman: C Text*. Their penitential frameworks, like the framework of Margery's *Book*, adopt the common medieval form of spiritual pilgrimage. The pilgrimage in both poems dramatizes the schism between "fallen" human notions of temporality and linear time, stressed by the poems' fictive autobiographical schemes, and the larger movement of Christian eschatology. Both poets mesh sacred and linear time, or individual experience, with Christian history in dramatic scriptural scenes that recall Franciscan participatory meditation. As in Margery's own personal narrative, both poems revise these gospel scenes and embellish them to reflect tension in the dreamers' spiritual psyches. Consequently, both works are meditations on "faith in the guise of an autobiography," reminding the reader that "one's own life has a part in the general redemptive pattern of history."[26]

[26] Carruthers, "Time, Apocalypse, and the Plot of *Piers Plowman*," pp. 176, 180.

16

In chapter 6, I return briefly to the literary context that first incorporated those elements that I have isolated and called "Franciscan" in reference to familiar English works or spiritual biographies. I explore how official Franciscan hagiography, Bonaventure's *Legenda maior*, evoked scriptural narrative to dramatize Francis's own life in thirteenth-century Umbria. In the fourteenth-century *Fioretti* the technique of joining visionary or imaginative experience with the authority of scripture, as seen in Franciscan meditation, presents critical questions about the fictional nature of these narratives. Franciscan biography is one prototype for the meditative spiritual autobiographies that emerged from an England evangelized by the Friars Minor and the Preaching Friars in the thirteenth century.

The Annunciation, MS Royal 2A, xviii, fol. 23ᵛ, by permission of the British Library.

2

Franciscan Meditation:
Historical and Literary Contexts

A great deal has been written about affective devotion and the function of meditational exercises devised for the English laity by medieval clerics and preachers in the form of lyrics, books of hours, and penitential manuals. As David Jeffrey suggests, however, affective piety and its penitential purpose cannot be examined adequately in any genre of religious literature outside the Franciscan devotional context that sustained and popularized vernacular penitential literature in thirteenth- and fourteenth-century England.[1] With respect to the pervasive Franciscan influence on late-medieval literature, John Fleming even claims:

> So far as the development of vernacular literature is concerned, the Franciscan influences were so various, and Franciscan mental habits so distinctive even among the mendicant orders, that it is useful to speak of a Franciscan literary style which was itself a part of the broader literary developments of the thirteenth and fourteenth centuries and an instrumental conduit through which stylistic change flowed into the vernacular continuum.[2]

In this chapter I explore a Franciscan meditative tradition that

[1] Jeffrey, *The Early English Lyric*, p. 321.
[2] Fleming, *An Introduction to the Franciscan Literature*, p. 239.

19

encouraged medieval laypersons to examine individual spirituality and culminated in a richly imaginative, intellectually provocative body of conversion literature that I call lay spiritual biography. With its focus on "perfect penance" and individual experience, Franciscan spirituality manifested itself most clearly in participatory meditations on Christ's humanity, best exemplified by the popular gospel harmonies. These meditative narratives asked the penitent not only to envision the pathetic course of Christ's life but also to consider simultaneously his or her own spiritual role in the historical scheme of salvation. The creative act of revising or reordering personal history in imitation of Christ's life is reminiscent of the conversional pattern of events imposed on medieval hagiography, for it schematizes disparate narratives into works purely about spiritual experience and hence transforms an otherwise disunified montage of events into spiritual autobiography or exemplary fiction.[3]

It may be difficult for us to examine this pious medieval habit of vicarious participation in gospel events. We can only estimate the spiritual satisfaction it provided for laypersons who eagerly sought religious experience to affirm their faith outside organized worship in which they had assumed at best only a peripheral role. This form of devotion, however, marks a fundamental historical and theological tie between affective piety and the developing sacrament of penance and is consequently a prominent factor in late-medieval penitential literature. By the middle of the thirteenth century the Franciscans had formally solidified this connection in Bonaventure's theology and in meditative works like the *Lignum vitae*, or *Tree of Life*, and the *Meditations on the Life of Christ*. Through such popular channels the English laity of the fourteenth century came to associate affective

---

[3] For an excellent discussion of the "relation of the imagination to historiography" in medieval biography see Judith H. Anderson, *Biographical Truth*, p. 4. Chapters 1 and 2, "Biographical Truth" and "Bede: Conventions of Portrayal," focus on the merging of fiction (which Anderson glosses as "the deliberate and creative shaping of fact") and history. In discussing the nature of "Truth" in medieval biography, Anderson concludes that exemplary narratives were "imaginatively and conceptually true — true not in opposition to factual, natural truth but quite often simply apart from it" (p. 22). In agreement with this observation, I define "exemplary fiction" as works that do not claim to be factually true but illustrate moral truths that are perhaps more central, and hence more real and of greater importance to the audience, than historicity.

devotion with the sacrament of penance and was conscious of the central role of the reformed will for spiritual health.

Robert Manning of Brunne's *Handlyng Synne*, the English translation of the *Manuel des pechiez*, indicates that by 1303 the English laity was well versed in the most salient tenets of institutionalized confession. The "fyrst poynt of shryft" in the text explains the spiritual and psychological foundation for the meditative exercises that we associate with mendicant pastoral activity and, indeed, late-medieval piety in general, whose aim is conversion of the hardened heart and its outward manifestation in the world:

> Þe fyrst poynt of þy shryfte oweþ to be,
> wi*th* þy gode wyl and herte fre,
> whan þou art in þy lyfe best,
> Awey þou shalt þy sy*n*ne kest;
> For þan wurschepest þou God above,
> And forsakest þy sy*n*ne for hys love.
> Davyd seyþ, yn wurde to fulfyl,
> God shrofe hy*m* wi*th* hys gode wyl.
> Abyde nat tyl þou most nedly;
> For þan hyt ys wi*th* fors and maystry;
> Þou shryvest þe þan for drede,
> Nat for love, but more for nede.[4]

The practice of confession, its method and purpose, was the subject of lengthy debates in the universities of Europe throughout the thirteenth century. Aquinas and Duns Scotus, among others, tried to systematize the sacramental penance that the Fourth Lateran Council made mandatory for laypersons once a year in its decree *Omnis utriusque sexus* of 1215. As Thomas Tentler explains, however, that was no simple task.[5] Throughout the Middle Ages penitential practices varied from region to region and often from parish to parish.[6] In *The Medieval Sinner*, Mary Flowers Braswell discusses sacramental penance and the development of a confessional literature in England. Her study

---

[4] Robert Manning of Brunne, *Handlyng Synne*, ed. Frederick J. Furnivall, p. 351.

[5] Thomas Tentler, *Sin and Confession on the Eve of the Reformation*, p. 51. See pp. 18–28 for a discussion of the development of contrition, confession, and absolution in the sacrament of penance. Also useful is chap. 7, "The Sacrament of Penance," in Greta Hort, *Piers Plowman and Contemporary Religious Thought*, pp. 130–55.

[6] Tentler, *Sin and Confession*, p. 30.

affirms that modern readers of works like *Piers Plowman* or Gower's *Confessio Amantis* can benefit from an introductory knowledge of the subtle distinctions theologians debated in creating a dogma for the new sacrament.[7] Of primary importance for our understanding of the affective nature of Franciscan devotion and the way it prepared the layperson for penance is the thirteenth-century controversy about "perfect" and "imperfect" penance, or "contrition" and "attrition."

The debate, largely conducted by Aquinas and Duns Scotus, tried to discern how much weight to give the priest's sacramental absolution when the penitent was "attrite" rather than "contrite."[8] The outcome of the argument for the history of sacramental penance is less important here than a knowledge of the distinctions between the degrees of contrition that it established and its subsequent influence on personal devotional practices.

A penitent who examined his or her conscience had to know not only the motive for the sins committed but also the motive for confessing. As the introductory passage from *Handlyng Synne* implies, sorrow arising from fear of punishment, or "drede," is "attrition," and thus repentance rooted in self-love and self-interest. Conversely, through contrition springing from a "fre heart," only for the love of God, the sin is graciously forgiven even before it is manifested in the sacrament of penance.[9]

Whether or not Francis was actually present at the Fourth Lateran Council — and he may well have been — his own life coincided with the development of a doctrine of penance in the Catholic church.[10] Francis's personal emphasis on the role of love and compassion in confession corresponded to the medieval church's eventual stand on degrees of

---

[7] Mary Flowers Braswell, *The Medieval Sinner*, p. 69. See chap. 3, "Confession as Characterization in the Literature of Fourteenth-Century England," pp. 61–100. Braswell's discussion of "The Genealogy of the Sinner: A Study in the Background of Penance," pp. 19–35, is also helpful in understanding how the institution of penance established a vocabulary that was later adopted in medieval literature dramatizing confession.

[8] Tentler, *Sin and Confession*, p. 26.

[9] Ibid., p. 27.

[10] Moorman, *A History of the Franciscan Order*, p. 29. Also see Rosalinde B. Brooke, "Papal Policy and the Fourth Lateran Council of 1215," in Brooke, trans. and ed., *The Coming of the Friars*, pp. 86–88.

penance. As we have seen in the *Testament*, Francis defined his very existence in terms of repentance and atonement. While there are often painful aspects of Francis's vehement rituals that strike the modern reader of his biographies as fanatical, medieval sources, particularly Bonaventure, celebrate the loving elements of his penitential fervor.

Francis received the stigmata, the physical token of his special sanctity, when he was retreating to Mount Alverna to fast and do penance for forty days in imitation of Christ. In his *Legenda maior*, or *Life of Francis*, Bonaventure establishes the importance of this miracle and its theological relevance to affective spirituality: "when the true love of Christ had transformed his lover into his image."[11] From a purely medieval perspective, Francis experienced the stigmata because he loved Christ in an unqualified, unconditional manner, untainted by human fear of sin and condemnation. Translated into Franciscan theology, this love becomes the catalyst for change and is the only source of Christian perfection, finding its human manifestation in "imitation" or Christ's image. Love is thus the impetus for necessary change, or conversion, initiating a new manner of external as well as internal conformity to Christ. Bonaventure views the stigmata as the fulfillment of Francis's first vision of the Crucifixion in his youth at San Damiano, where, simple and untried in the ways of faith, he had a vision of the cross that led him away from his comfortable, secular life. In chapter 13 of the *Legenda maior*, Bonaventure explains that Francis's stigmata are the external sign of a life of perfect imitation: "For he had wisely learned so to divide the time given him for merit that he expended part of it in working for his neighbor's benefit and devoted the other part to the perfect ecstasy of contemplation."[12]

The "Fire of Love" that Francis received, which became a prominent motif in English mystical writing, was the reward for a perfect love of Christ crucified, hence for "contrition." While affective devotion did

---

[11] Bonaventure, *The Life of Francis*, in *Works*, trans. and ed. Cousins, p. 307. The Latin passage reads: "Postquam igitur verus Christi amor in eandem imaginem transformavit amantem." Bonaventure, *Legenda maior*, chap. 13, par. 5, p. 543.

[12] Bonaventure, *Life of St. Francis*, in *Works*, trans. and ed. Cousins, p. 303. The Latin reads: "Nam tempus sibi concessum ad meritum dividere sic prudenter didicerat, ut aliud proximorum lucris laboriosis impenderet, aliud contemplationis tranquillis excessibus dedicaret." Bonaventure, *Legenda maior*, chap. 13, par. 1, p. 542.

not originate with Francis, the Franciscans made the experience of the Passion, and the appropriate response thereto, the center of their affective penitential theology. Francis's conversion, motivated by love and compassion, exemplified perfect penance for thirteenth- and fourteenth-century laypersons. Doubtless his mercantile origins and his unextraordinary early life made his conversion all the more remarkable and inspiring for lay penitents. It is hardly surprising that Franciscan theology and the penitential literature that emerged from it were permeated by an affective strain of devotion or by imagery that primarily intended to evoke feelings of pity and love leading to "perfect" penance.

Throughout the twelfth and thirteenth centuries religious writers in England evoked images of Christ's life in private meditations.[13] Godric of Finchale, Aelred (or Ethelred), Adam of Dryburgh, Stephen of Sawley, and Edmund of Abingdon are noted for their Christocentric spirituality. All focused on the mysteries of the incarnation as effective preparation for prayer and spiritual cleansing. Elizabeth Salter, who has written extensively on private meditation on Christ's humanity in monastic England, points out that the Franciscans were responsible for recasting such private devotions into a recognizable "literary formula" for the laity.[14] While Bonaventure surely derived personal spiritual satisfaction from composing the *Lignum vitae*, "the regulation of the material has been carried out in an effort to draw deeper compassion from the reader—the first fruit of meditation."[15]

Through meditative narratives, various gospel harmonies like the *Meditations on the Life of Christ*, the Franciscans established an oral, visual, and written tradition of systematized devotions on Christ's humanity in the context of his historical life. Franciscan meditation, as we shall see, urged the penitent to visualize gospel events dramatically, or imaginatively to re-create gospel narrative extemporaneously. The Franciscans found Christocentric meditation useful preparation for prayer and the sacrament of penance because it required only that the spiritual novice be familiar with scriptural stories.

[13] James Walsh, *Pre-Reformation English Spirituality*, p. ix.
[14] Salter, *Nicholas Love's* Myrrour, p. 143. For a detailed catalogue and description of English meditative lives of Christ, see ibid., chap. 5, pp. 119–78.
[15] Ibid., p. 143.

Nonetheless, Christocentric devotion is often erroneously regarded as a simple or sentimental gaze on the concrete life of Jesus. In the narrative pattern of the *Meditations* Christ's temporal life is presented as a dramatic pilgrimage toward Jerusalem, where his own final conversion, or surrendering of the will, is manifested by the Passion, which fully unveils to the world his dual nature. A close look at the legends or nonscriptural materials in this overtly Franciscan manuscript indicates that the embellishment of gospel events by penitents evoked a more familiar, accessible world and thus allowed them to engage in very human speculation about Christ's nature. The experience of meditation thus became a means of knowing God. Whether or not meditative narratives were efficacious prepenitential exercises depended on the penitent's ability to experience gospel events vicariously without losing sight of his or her own sinful life. The penitential act is successful when an individual selectively evaluates personal history with contrition as the final end. The process of imposing a "moral design" on the past to schematize temporal life into a "true, eternal pattern of conversion" is essentially the function of spiritual biography, best exemplified in Augustine's *Confessions*.[16]

In *The Forms of Autobiography*, William Spengemann explains that "confession is no longer a revelation of the self to God, who already knows everything, but a revelation of the self to the self, an act of self-knowledge, a process of discovering the true meaning of one's life."[17] Francis's own conversion and struggle to order his life in the pattern of *imitatio* provided by Scripture are acknowledged in the *Testament* as a process of self-discovery. Franciscan meditation functions similarly, offering Christ's life as the prototypical pattern of conversion and encouraging laypersons to use imagination and vision to penetrate hearts and minds clouded by sin.

Franciscan meditation was effective, then, not only because it taught salvation history but also because it reaffirmed principles of belief for the single penitent as a private religious experience. Christocentric meditation in a narrative framework presented history as a divine plan unfolding in temporal time and space, one in which all Christians

[16] William Spengemann, *The Forms of Autobiography*, p. 1.
[17] Ibid., p. 5.

participate from creation to the Last Judgment. When a penitent created scenes from the gospel — "ghostly" sights that increased faith and confirmed this deliberate order — the experience was valid proof of a cosmic scheme that promised individual salvation and, more immediately, provided daily life with a conscious pattern of redemption. In this manner the meditator's imaginative experience buttressed the order celebrated collectively in the sacramental religious worship of the liturgical year. Rather than contradicting each other, history and spirituality arrived at the same end, albeit through different means.[18]

We may question the nature of visions and meditations that provided vicarious religious experience, whether they were considered divinely inspired or were conjured imaginatively. Ultimately, however, the important question for the penitent in fourteenth-century England was whether or not the meditative vision provided a sufficiently moving experience to incite sorrow and lead to conversion. The ontological nature of the vision is less crucial for our understanding of late-medieval spirituality. Unlike the English mystics, such as Julian of Norwich and the author of *The Cloud of Unknowing*, both of whom cautiously discuss the origins of visions that purport to be heavenly revelations, those who practice Franciscan meditation consciously initiate visions with the very specific purpose of penance in mind. To confuse mystical or beatific vision with meditative vision, as readers often do with *The Book of Margery Kempe*, for example, leads to misinterpretation of the text. While Margery insists that she has beatific or divinely granted visions like those experienced by Julian of Norwich, nearly all her visions are scripturally based and hence clearly meditative.

An examination of Bonaventure's *Lignum vitae*, the earliest and most influential source of Franciscan devotions based on Christ's life, may illuminate the development of visual meditation. Among his most lyrical works, the *Lignum* voices all the sentiments that pervade late-medieval piety. In considering the agony of the Crucifixion, Bonaventure stresses that compassion (*compassio*) should be the penitent's response to Christ's suffering, for only compassion can move the hardened sinner to compunction: "And you, lost man, the cause of all this

---

[18] Pierre Pourrat, *Christian Spirituality in the Middle Ages*, 1:188.

confusion and sorrow, how is it that you do not break down and weep?"[19]

Saint Bonaventure's affective theology reflects a deep awareness of the natural role that our sensuous faculties can play in spiritual growth.[20] We cannot dissociate the primacy of vision and imagination in his thinking from the later tendency in popular Franciscan spirituality, whether manifested in lyrics, drama, or meditation, to use images and create scenarios in arousing sorrow. Nor can we fully understand the rationale for later devotional works that fix the meditator's attention on the grotesquely realistic details of the Passion without first considering the intellectual and devotional foundation that Bonaventure established incorporating the naturalistic, poetic elements of Francis's own spirituality.

Threatened by Joachimism, the Franciscan order selected Bonaventure as minister-general in 1257. Bonaventure, who was moderate in his interpretation of the Franciscan Rule, acknowledged the difficulties in strictly adhering to Francis's adamant desire for absolute poverty in view of the order's unwieldy expansion. He was, nonetheless, deeply devoted to Francis's ideals.[21] Bonaventure's writings during the period of his tenure reflect a personal search for an understanding of Francis's life; the *Legenda maior* is the purest expression of Francis's exemplary role as the perfect pilgrim, whose life of daily conformity to Christ became legendary during his own lifetime. Bonaventure not only schematizes Francis's life according to hagiographic models that stress conversion and miracles with an eye on heavenly glory but also consistently affirms that true *imitatio* in the world leads to profound mystical revelation, such as Francis's stigmata. The *Itinerarium mentis in Deum* similarly illustrates Bonaventure's vision of spiritual ecstasy as the end of a process of purgation, illumination, and perfection. His biography of Francis, following this design, interprets Francis's life as the paradigm of spiritual journey in Bonaventure's speculative theology.

[19] Bonaventure, *The Tree of Life*, in *Works*, trans. and ed. Cousins, p. 146. The Latin reads: "Et tu, perdite homo, totius confusionis et contritionis huius causa existens, quomodo non in fletum foras erumpis?" Bonaventure, *Lignum vitae*, chap. 6, par. 24, p. 77.

[20] Etienne Gilson, *The Philosophy of St. Bonaventure*, p. 323. See chap. 12, "The Illumination of the Intellect," pp. 309–64.

[21] Moorman, *A History of the Franciscan Order*, p. 152.

The *Lignum vitae*, the third important work of this period, is equally imbued with Franciscan spirituality as Bonaventure sensitively perceived it. The work is essentially a spiritual biography of Christ's life, composed as a series of dramatic meditations. In keeping with the moral or didactic function of meditation, Bonaventure creates an allegory for Christ's historical life. The twelve fruits that hang from the branches of the "imaginary tree" of life provide the moral nourishment necessary for each Christian.[22]

Bonaventure's purpose in combining meditation with sequential narrative is clearly affective, or experiential. He emphasizes the common fabric of Christ's life through concrete, detailed description to establish a bond of humanity between man and God. By directly urging the reader or meditator to envision specific biblical scenes, Bonaventure dramatically evokes the compassion and wonder that provide the emotional response necessary for conversion. His schematic, poetic treatment of Christ's life stimulated an artistic movement that eventually spread Franciscan devotional elements and interpretations, and particularly imaginative meditation, throughout Europe.[23] In reference to the numerous illuminated psalters possessed by the nobility in late-medieval England, for example, Douglas Gray speculates that "the wish of the owners for a deeper and more emotional participation in the sacred events depicted on the pages may reflect the influence of confessors from the new mendicant orders."[24]

In the *Lignum vitae*, Bonaventure fashions brief but vivid tableaux, or iconographic representations, of Christ's life as the focal points of meditation. Recognizing that the spiritual beginner, like Francis, has natural limitations, Bonaventure does not avoid visualization as a spiritual tool but claims in the Prologue of his work that, "since imagination aids understanding, I have arranged in the form of an

[22] Bonaventure, *The Tree of Life*, in *Works*, trans. and ed. Cousins, p. 120. The Latin reads: "in imaginaria quadam arbore." Bonaventure, *Lignum vitae*, prol., par. 2, p. 68.

[23] David Wilkins, "The Meaning of Space in Fourteenth-Century Tuscan Painting," in David Jeffrey, ed., *By Things Seen: Reference and Recognition in Medieval Thought*, p. 118. Wilkins explains the imaginative technique of the *Meditations on the Life of Christ* and its connection to the "growing valuation of the depiction of natural reality in painting" in trecento art (pp. 118–21).

[24] Douglas Gray, *Themes and Images in the Medieval Religious Lyric*, p. 22.

imaginary tree the few items I have collected from among many."[25] By "imagination," however, Bonaventure means not our modern concept of imagination, with its implications of fanciful creation or active fiction making, but the medieval definition of imagination: the "passive" cognitive faculty that retains the forms of visible things for recollection and thus cooperates with reason to comprehend phenomena.[26] Sensible impressions are "preserved in the imagination, the *virtus imaginaria*, a kind of treasury and storehouse of the sensible species."[27] When the intellect, through an act of the will, wishes to recall images for examination, as in the imaginative representation of meditation, it must necessarily depend on the imagination that passively preserves them. Only memory, however, can actively recall them. Unlike the imagination, memory "is capable of reminiscence, that is of recalling to consciousness."[28] Both faculties, however, perform their tasks when an individual wishes to recollect the experiences and thoughts that constitute biography, or embellish a scene from scripture with details from personal experience.

In the *Lignum vitae*, Bonaventure reconstructs episodes of the Gospels to imprint (*imprimere*) them on the penitent's memory (*memoria*) for future recollection.[29] Each scene is an abbreviated narrative, a summary rather than an extract from the Gospels phrased simply but vividly to call images to memory. These narrative sections, analogous to "compositions" in meditative lyrics, precede emotional responses to the scenes that are transformed into a series of lyrical prayers ending with a petition. While Bonaventure's work is elegant, and intended for a highly literate or clerical audience, we can see how this meditative structure could be adapted for the literate, and even illiterate, layperson, who could recall the images and experience the scenes unhampered by the commentary Bonaventure adds to his text.

Of chief importance for the development of Franciscan meditation is

[25] Bonaventure, *The Tree of Life*, in *Works*, trans. and ed. Cousins, p. 120. The Latin reads: "Et quonian imaginatio iuvat intelligentiam, ideo quae ex multis pauca collegi in imaginaria quadam arbore." Bonaventure, *Lignum vitae*, prol., par. 2, p. 68.

[26] Gilson, *The Philosophy of St. Bonaventure*, p. 327.

[27] Ibid., p. 327.

[28] Ibid., p. 328.

[29] Bonaventure, *The Tree of Life*, in *Works*, trans. and ed. Cousins, p. 119. For the Latin see Bonaventure, *Lignum vitae*, prol., para. 2, p. 68.

the way Bonaventure urges the meditator to participate in the devotions like an actor assuming a role in a drama. Most of the compositions conclude with a direct invocation to the reader to enter imaginatively into the narrative, actively responding to each scene. Bonaventure asks us to accompany the three Kings and become a first witness of the Epiphany: "Do not now turn away from the brilliance of that star in the east which guides you. Become a companion of the holy Kings."[30] In the chapters following, Bonaventure bids us to hold the infant Jesus and rejoice with Anna when Mary comes to meet her. We are to flee into Egypt with them and later help Mary seek her son, teaching in the temple. The meditations thus mimetically reinforce the gospel stories in their proper sequence. This is particularly obvious in Margery Kempe's visual meditation, where we sense that she has internalized, or dramatically realized, the urgency of the flight after the Epiphany: "& soon aftyr cam an awngel & bad owyr Lady & Ioseph gon / fro þe cuntre ob [*sic*] Bedlem in-to Egypt. Þan went þis creatur forth wyth owyr Lady, day be day purveyng his herborw wyth gret reverens."[31]

Margery shapes her meditations in a spatial and temporal framework, emphasizing her service to the holy family when they are most needy. This is in keeping with Bonaventure's encouragement to suffer with Christ. We are reminded in the *Lignum* that Jesus initiated his public ministry with penance in the desert; to appreciate this sacrifice the penitent too must "become a companion of wild beasts" and an "imitator and sharer of the hidden silence, the devout prayer, the daylong fasting."[32] Francis and Bonaventure and medieval penitents like Margery Kempe imitated Christ, physically climbing Mount Alverna or laboriously ascending "þe Mouwnt Qwarentyne þer owyr Lord

---

[30] Bonaventure, *The Tree of Life*, in *Works*, trans. and ed. Cousins, p. 130. The Latin reads: "Noli iam et tu ab illius orientis et praeeuntis stellae declinare fulgore, quin potius, sacrorum regum comes effectus." Bonaventure, *Lignum vitae*, chap. 2, par. 8, p. 72.

[31] Margery Kempe, *The Book of Margery Kempe*, ed. Sanford Brown Meech, with notes and appendices by Hope Emily Allen, p. 19, lines 33–34. All further quotations from this work are taken from this edition.

[32] Bonaventure, *The Tree of Life*, in *Works*, trans. and ed. Cousins, p. 134. The Latin reads: "Eia nunc Christi discipule, cum pio magistro solitudinis secreta perquire, ut socius ferarum effectus, arcani silentii, orationis devotae, disturni ieiunii." Bonaventure, *Lignum vitae*, chap. 3, par. 10, p. 73.

fastyd fowrty days."[33] These actions complement the meditative exercises that Bonaventure wrote and emphasize the necessity of remembering continually Christ's humanity and our own willful oblivion to his suffering. In the *Lignum* we assume the role of fearful Peter and are directly addressed as disciples, or we become the thief on the cross. As unredeemed participants, we become acutely sensitive to the power of vicarious experience as a means of effecting change:

> O my God, good Jesus, although I am in every way without merit and unworthy, grant to me, who did not merit to be present at these events in the body, that I may ponder them faithfully in my mind, and experience toward you, my God crucified and put to death for me, that feeling of compassion which your innocent mother and the penitent Magdalene experienced at the very hour of your passion.[34]

Through dramatic enactments of Christ's life Bonaventure enables the sinner to travel in Christ's company and experience his perfect charity, as did Francis. He underlines the didactic or moral theme of conformity in the opening lines, heightening the Franciscan nature of the meditations: "With Christ I am nailed to the cross." The *Lignum* is not only a spiritual biography of Christ but an imaginative pilgrimage whose aim is conversion and self-revelation for the reader.

Of course, the metaphor of pilgrimage as spiritual journey is not singularly Franciscan; the rhythm of Christian life has always assumed a narrative structure of journey and reconciliation.[35] Since Augustine's *Confessions*, "conversion signified the very moment of enlightenment, whereby a blind, stumbling and a vagrant wandering about could be converted into a fully purposeful pilgrimage, a *peregrinatio* homeward."[36] The double nature of the Franciscan life of which John Fleming speaks, however, gives this journey an equally literal and

[33] Kempe, *The Book of Margery Kempe*, p. 74, lines 9–10.

[34] Bonaventure, *The Tree of Life*, in *Works*, trans. and ed. Cousins, p. 158. The Latin reads: "Deus meus, bone Iesu, concede mihi quamquam per omnem modum immerito et indigno, ut qui corpore his interesse non merui, fideli tamen haec eadem mente pertractans, illum ad te Deum meum pro me crucifixum et mortuum compassionis affectum experiar, quem innocens Mater tua et poenitens Magdalena in ipsa passionis tuae hora senserunt." Bonaventure, *Lignum vitae*, chap. 8, par. 32, p. 80.

[35] Carruthers, "Time, Apocalypse, and the Plot of *Piers Plowman*," p. 188.

[36] Karl Joachim Weintraub, *The Value of the Individual: Self and Circumstance in Autobiography*, p. 37.

figurative nature in Franciscan meditative works fashioned as spiritual biography.

It is this conscious meshing of the inner and outer, which assumed primary significance in Francis's conception of the order, that permeates all Franciscan thought and hence Franciscan devotional habits. It is also this marriage of the spiritual with the physical, or the mimetic, that proved so appealing to laypersons in its simplified forms. Franciscan devotion acknowledged subjective experience as a bridge to God, approving a measure of autonomy in the religious practices of the laity that had previously been a mark of spiritual elitism. Rather than having its roots in a popular ignorance or religious sentimentalism, this "subjectivism" in affective piety corresponds to a strain of "late medieval philosophy marked by a rigorous empiricism."[37] Certainly Bonaventure's own thirteenth-century philosophical and theological works express a similar interest in a faith and an epistemology grounded in experience.

As a result, both the *Itinerarium* and the *Lignum vitae* display a reverence for Francis's ability to embrace the created universe, the human realm of experience, as a vestige of divine order. One of the most attractive characteristics of Franciscan spirituality is its fundamental sympathy for the human condition: until death we are inextricably earthbound. The human plight is to be "clad in clot," as the *Pearl* dreamer mournfully laments after his daughter's death.[38] Francis himself humorously alluded to this burden of a mortal body as "Brother Ass."[39] Yet since they lived not only the contemplative life but also the *via activa*, serving the poor in the world, neither Francis nor his followers could adhere to the monastic contempt for physical creation.

Instead, in the *Itinerarium*, Bonaventure reasserts the Augustinian idea that experience of the sensible world is a natural and primary step toward God. Chapter 2 invokes the metaphor of God as craftsman, whose essence manifests itself in the mirror of creation. Sensible reminders of the Creator, called exemplars, could be "presented to souls still untrained and immersed in sensible things, so that through

[37] Gray, *Themes and Images*, p. 28.

[38] *Pearl*, ed. E. V. Gordon, p. 1, line 22. All further quotations from *Pearl* are taken from this edition.

[39] Bonaventure, *Legenda*, chap. 2, par. 1, p. 508. The Latin reads: "Unde corpus suum fratrem asinum apellabat, tanquam laboriosis supponendum oneribus."

sensible things which they see they will be carried over to intelligible things which they do not see as through signs to what is signified."[40] Franciscan meditations, consequently, function on a mimetic principle, offering vision and tangible experience recalled from memory as the spiritual child's first step toward God.

Bonaventure's speculative interpretation of this basic human desire for ocular proof, or experience of God's redemptive plan, is translated dramatically into Franciscan lyrics and late-medieval drama like the Corpus Christi cycles which were heavily influenced by Franciscan evangelism. Auerbach reminds us in *Mimesis* that this "Franciscan power of expression led to a . . . more direct and intense representation of human events" than hitherto expressed in Western devotional works.[41] The incarnational elements of Franciscan meditation and dramatic interpretations of scriptural scenes that result from freedom of imagination provide a curious "embedding of the sublime and sacred event in a reality which is simultaneously contemporary . . . and omnitemporal."[42]

How could Bonaventure forget that his beloved Francis, when he was first commanded by God to "repair my House," literally heaved stones and mortar about for some time, intending to repair San Damiano "materially"?[43] In the *Legenda maior*, Bonaventure develops Francis's search for his private role in salvation history according to the pattern he created in the *Itinerarium* as representative of all human growth toward God. At first Francis, like all other sinners, "had no experience in interpreting divine mysteries, nor did he know how to pass through the visible images to grasp the invisible truth beyond."[44] Bonaventure

[40] Bonaventure, *The Soul's Journey into God*, in *Works*, trans. and ed. Cousins, p. 76. The Latin reads: "quae, inquam, sunt exemplaria vel potius exemplata, proposita mentibus adhuc rudibus et sensibilius, ut per sensibilia, quae vident, transferantur ad intelligibilia, quae non vident, tanquam per signa ad signata." Bonaventure, *Itinerarium*, chap. 2, par., 11, p. 302.

[41] Auerbach, *Mimesis*, p. 170.

[42] Ibid., p. 172.

[43] Bonaventure, *The Life of Francis*, in *Works*, ed. and trans. Cousins, p. 191. The Latin reads: "Totum se recolligit ad mandantum de materiali ecclesia reparandra, licet principalior intentio verbi ad eam ferretur, quam Christus suo sanguine acquisivit." Bonaventure, *Legenda*, chap. 2, par. 1, p. 508.

[44] Bonaventure, *The Life of Francis*, in *Works*, trans. and ed. Cousins, p. 188. The Latin reads: "Evigilans itaque mane, cum nondum haberet exercitatum animum ad

indicates both the insubstantial nature of earthly phenomena and God's role as supreme craftsman in the *Itinerarium* by calling sensible reminders of his presence in the world "umbrae, resonantiae et picturae."[45] Bonaventure's choice of words reveals that in his complex expression of spiritual experience he, like other medieval mystics, acknowledges our limited vocabulary, based on ephemeral temporal experience. Nonetheless, Bonaventure sympathetically creates images of Christ's life in the meditations of the *Lignum vitae*, affirming the need of the spiritual novice to approach God from the familiar context of the sensible world.

Bonaventure's meditative technique proved so successful that throughout the Middle Ages meditative texts characterized by imaginative, visual appeals were assumed to be his work. The most widely disseminated Franciscan work in the Middle Ages, for example, the *Meditations on the Life of Christ*, was attributed to Bonaventure because, like the *Lignum*, it demanded an imaginative, emotional response to detailed descriptions of Gospel events.[46] Like the *Lignum*, one-third of which elaborates the Crucifixion scenes from the Gospel, the *Meditations* is also characterized by its typically Franciscan emphasis on the Passion. In contrast to the brief *Lignum*, however, which is circumscribed by Bonaventure's theological perspective, the *Meditations* is a compendium of popular medieval beliefs, some adapted directly from scripture, others borrowed from the church fathers, Bernard of Clairvaux, or pseudo-Gospels such as *Nicodemus*.

The *Meditations on the Life of Christ* is thought to have been composed by a Franciscan, Giovanni de San Gimignano, during the second half of the thirteenth century.[47] There are still a number of uncertainties concerning both authorship and date, but they are largely irrelevant for our purposes. While it is criticized for its sentimentalism, its fanciful treatment of scripture, and its ungainly structure, the *Meditations* had an immediate impact on art, literature, and

---

divina perscrutanda mysteria nesciretque per visibilium species transire ad contuendam invisibilium veritatem." Bonaventure, *Legenda maior*, chap. 1, par. 3, p. 506.

[45] Bonaventure, *Itinerarium*, chap. 2, par. 11, p. 302.

[46] Salter, *Nicholas Love's* Myrrour, p. 124.

[47] Derek Brewer, *English Gothic Literature*, p. 254.

devotional practices in England and on the Continent.[48] Its graphically detailed illustrations of daily life inspired translations into the vernacular in many languages. Its literary prominence is demonstrated by the fact that there are more than two hundred extant copies, several of which have picture cycles.[49]

The Passion cycle from the *Meditations* (which came to be called the *Pseudo-Bonaventure* in the eighteenth century, when scholars marked the disparity between Bonaventure's style and that of this gospel harmony), was translated into English verse as early as 1338 in the *Meditations on the Supper of Our Lord*. The *Supper*, also assigned to Bonaventure, was clearly intended to be read or recited before an audience, further establishing the work's centrality in a meditative and literary tradition. According to Salter, seven separate translations of the Passion section of the *Meditations on the Life of Christ* were made during the fourteenth century in England.[50]

The purpose of the *Meditations*, like that of the *Lignum*, is to transform the penitent into an apostle, a Magdalene, or a Francis, to whom the manuscript specifically refers in the Prologue. Even the earlier versions of this text, which were not consciously edited for the laity, as was Nicholas Love's fifteenth-century translation, reveal the essentially popular nature of Franciscan devotion. Although written for a Poor Clare who lived enclosed according to the rule composed by Saint Francis for the sister order, the *Meditations* does not direct itself solely toward the enclosed, as do many of the earlier versions of the *Ancrene Riwle*. Rather than denigrate the active life, it acknowledges the purgative stage as a spiritual infancy through which all Christians must pass, whether lay or religious. Above all else, the *Meditations*

---

[48] Bonaventure, *Works*, trans. and ed. Cousins, p. 12. Also see M[ary] Jordan Stallings, *Meditaciones de Passione Christi olim Sancto Bonaventurae attributae*, pp. 34–35. Stallings notes the stylistic differences between the *Lignum* and the *Meditaciones* and explains that, unlike Bonaventure, whose scholastic writings display a skillful knowledge of Latin grammar and rhetoric, the author of the *Meditaciones* "conceived his work in Italian, and hence the latent structure of the rapidly flowing vernacular is everywhere evident."

[49] *Meditations on the Life of Christ*, trans. and ed. Ragusa and Greene. See introduction, p. xxiii.

[50] Salter, *Nicholas Love's* Myrrour, p. 103.

proposes *imitatio* as the path of righteous living in keeping with Franciscan spirituality:

> What do the Holy Apostles teach us? . . . Not to read Plato or confound ourselves in the depths of Aristotle, not always to learn and at no time to arrive at the knowledge of truth. They teach me to live. Do you think that it is a small thing to know how to live? It is a great thing, and even the greatest.[51]

The author consistently stresses the importance of experiencing gospel events as a means of knowing, rather than relying on the traditional authorities established through medieval monasticism. The Franciscan assures the Poor Clare that she has sufficient knowledge to benefit from such devotions:

> Therefore you ought to know that it is enough to meditate only on what the Lord did or what happened concerning him, or on what is told according to the Gospel stories, feeling yourself present in those places as if things were done in your presence, as it comes directly to your soul in thinking of them.[52]

Clearly this distinction between "learning" and a "knowledge of truth," between a formal knowledge and an internalized, experiential knowledge, has vital implications for our understanding of Franciscan and hence medieval devotions. As previously discussed, Franciscan devotion was not precluded by literacy or even a fundamental knowledge of Catholic dogma. It was accessible to any person who knew the Gospels — the teaching of which, in conjunction with the teaching of penance, was the chief mission of the Franciscan evangelical program. Franciscan meditation thus opened up a new kind of personal spiritual exercise to a long-deprived group of Catholics, especially the uneducated laity. The *Meditations* not only acknowledged but also encouraged an individual approach in visualizing gospel scenes. As we have

---

[51] *Meditations on the Life of Christ*, trans. and ed. Ragusa and Green, p. 255. The Latin reads: "Quid igitur docuerunt, vel docent nos sancti apostoli? . . . non sempere discere, et nunquam ad veritatis scientiam pervenire. Docuerunt me vivere. Putas, parva res sit scire vivere? Magnum aliquid, imo maximum." *Meditationes*, ed. Peltier, chap. 48, p. 574.

[52] *Meditations on the Life of Christ*, trans. and ed. Ragusa and Green, p. 387. The Latin reads: "Igitur scire debes, quod meditari sufficit solum factum quod Dominus fecit vel circa eum contigit fieri vel dici secundum historiam evangelicam, te ibidem praesentem exhibendo, ac si in tua praesentia fierent, prout simpliciter animo in dictis cogitanti occurrit." *Meditationes*, ed. Peltier, chap. 11, p. 629.

seen, this is typical of Franciscan life, but that this freedom of prayer life was extended to laypersons as well as to the friars themselves reflects the truly radical nature of Francis's accomplishments.

Imaginative freedom is exhibited in both the meditations and the pictures that accompany them. Isa Ragusa and Rosalie Green have noted the unusual "number and density of pictures" in the illustrated manuscripts of the *Meditations* they examined in preparation for their much-needed translation of a vernacular version.[53] Many of the gospel episodes that had previously received little or no attention from manuscript illuminators were energetically expanded in their text "with an illustration for each moment of the action."[54] As a result, the narrative is conveyed in an almost cinematographic manner and includes startling details from everyday life. They note, for example, that the wedding at Cana has been expanded to twelve pictures from the one traditional scene of the Virgin instructing the servants to follow her son's commands. They appropriately conclude that the "artists must have enjoyed a certain freedom from traditional modes" of visual representation.[55] We cannot divorce this creative act from the meditative process itself, which embellishes the Gospels by fleshing out the skeletal narratives with details from life experiences.

"Imaginative freedom" certainly harkens back to Bonaventure's belief that memory's ability to recollect and focus on meaningful images aids understanding, but in the *Meditations* the emphasis on a personal relationship with Christ takes precedence over strict adherence to the Gospels. In fact, in the *Meditations*, although imagination still refers to visualization or recollection, the rudiments of fiction as we know it are certainly present. The *Meditations* legitimizes the re-creation of gospel events, and even supplemental or fictional events, if it increases devotion. The issue is not whether such occurrences actually happened but whether they are morally "true" and thus fulfill the primary function of meditation — to teach us how to live. To this end the author warns his pupil at the beginning of the *Meditations* that she is not to

[53] *Meditations on the Life of Christ*, trans. and ed. Ragusa and Green. See introduction, p. xxx.
[54] Ibid., p. xxx.
[55] Ibid., p. xxx.

quibble about sources or distinguish between the literal story and its imaginative interpretation:

> However, you must not believe that all things said and done by Him on which we may meditate are known to us in writing. For the sake of greater impressiveness I shall tell them to you as they might have occurred according to the devout belief of the imagination and the varying interpretation of the mind. It is possible to contemplate, explain, and understand the Scriptures in as many ways as we consider necessary, and in such a manner as not to contradict the truth of life and justice and not to oppose faith and morality. Thus, when you find it said here, "this was said and done by the Lord Jesus" and by others of whom we read, if it cannot be demonstrated by the Scriptures, you must consider it only as a requirement of devout contemplation.[56]

The author of the *Meditations* is thus perfectly aware of his embellishments and is careful to qualify his definition of *imaginarias repraesentationes* noted in the previous passage. To profit morally from the meditations, the reader does not have to locate their source in scripture, but must re-create and imaginatively participate in the gospel scenes. Rather than worry his reader about the orthodoxy or the factual premise of the experience, he advises her to "take it as if I had said 'Suppose that this is what the Lord Jesus said and did.'"[57] The key word in the Latin is *meditari*, which means "to consider" or "to meditate"[58] but clearly suggests something akin to "to suppose," as does the author's later use of *interponere*: "Here one may interpolate a very beautiful

---

[56] Ibid., p. 5. The Latin reads: "Non autem credas, quod omnia quae [a] ipsum dixisse, vel fecisse constat, meditari possimus, vel quod omnia scripta sint: ego vero ad majorem impressionem, ea sic, *ac si ita fuissant*, narrabo, prout contigere vel contigisse credi possunt, secundum quasdam *imaginarias repraesentationes*, quas animus diversimode percipit. Nam et circa divinam Scripturam meditari, exponere et intelligere multifarie, prout expendire credimus, possumus, dummondo no sit contra veritatem vitae, justitiae et doctrinae, et non sit contra fidem et contra bonos mores. Cum autem me narrantem invenies: "Ita dixit vel fecit Dominus Jesus," seu alia, quae introducuntur; si illud per Scripturam probari non possit, non aliter accipias, quam devota meditatio exigit." Prologue, *Meditationes*, ed. Peltier, p. 511. Italics added.

[57] *Meditations on the Life of Christ*, trans. and ed. Ragusa and Green, p. 5. The Latin reads: "Hoc est, perinde accipe, ac si dicerem: Mediteris quod ita dixit vel fecit Dominus Jesus; et sic de similibus." Prologue, *Meditationes*, ed. Peltier, p. 511.

[58] *Oxford Latin Dictionary* (1982), "Meditari," p. 1090. Also see *interponere*, p. 946. The *OLD* glosses *interponere* variously as "to insert (in a temporal or other series)" and "to interpose." Also see R. E. Latham, *Revised Medieval Latin Word List* (London: Oxford University Press, 1965), p. 256. Latham glosses *interpolatio* as "to interrupt."

meditation of which the Scripture does not speak."[59] Interestingly, while the classical definition of *interponere* is "to put in," it also means "to introduce as a witness or participant."[60] Its medieval counterpart, however, is *interpolare*. While the verb *interpolare* conveys the meaning "to interpose," an "interpolator" may also be a falsifier, or creator of conscious fictions.[61] This may explain the author's anxious care to use qualifiers like *perinde*. His primary concern is not to adhere to the literal truth of the Gospels, although he firmly stresses that he is presenting not false doctrine but the *veritatem vitae*. He is offering not myths but likelihoods, and their function is to appeal to the *bonos mores* of his reader by presenting a more humane picture of the Savior. In reading meditative texts, we must carefully distinguish the difference between supposition as a carefully defined devotional technique and scriptural glosses that claim to be factual, rather than simply moral truths.

In her study of the *Meditaciones de Passione Christi*, one manuscript of the Passion sequence in the *Meditations*, Sister Mary Jordan Stallings points out that the author "makes no attempt at precision" in translating the scriptural passages "and very likely quotes the shorter passages from memory."[62] She speculates that, for the most part, the *Meditations* in its various translations and manuscripts consciously drew its audience from the laity, and hence its translators made little effort to be precise. They were more concerned with appealing to the emotions through recognizable scenes and images.[63] She also notes the freedom of tense and grammatical structure in the treatise, which recalls Auerbach's discussion of Francis's experiential prose. She was struck, for example, by "the effective use of the historical present in the narration. This coupled with a paratactic sentence structure produces the effect of

---

[59] *Meditations on the Life of Christ*, trans. and ed. Ragusa and Green, p. 308. The Latin reads: "Hic potest interponi meditatio valde pulchra, de qua tamen Scriptura non loquitur." *Meditationes*, ed. Peltier. chap. 72, p. 595.

[60] *OLD*, s.v. *Interponere*, no. 8, p. 946.

[61] J. F. Niermeyer, *Mediae latinitatis lexicon minus* (Leiden: E. J. Brill, 1976), p. 551. *Interpolare* is glossed here as "to interpose, interrupt"; *interpolator*, however, is glossed as "falsifier."

[62] Stallings, *Meditaciones*, p. 15.

[63] Ibid., p. 24.

an eyewitness account of the scenes portrayed."[64] Also like Francis's prose is the "frequent use of et at the beginning of sentences, and the lack of balance and interplay of sentence structure," all of which share the quality of the parabolic prose in the Gospels.[65] It is not unusual that such Franciscan narratives should attempt to evoke the parables in the Gospels, for these Franciscan stories took their authority from the dramatization of the moral choices that confront sinful humanity in Jesus's own tales. The spirit of the *Meditations*, as of Christ's own parables, embraces the Christian's ability to interpret the law for righteous living, often at the expense of the facts that constitute law.

In his discussion of the tradition of affective devotion and meditation in England, James Walsh notes that this creative treatment of biblical events is less prevalent in Anglo-Saxon England.[66] While the Franciscans freely wove legends and tales of the Virgin in Marian devotions, relying minimally on the scant information in the Gospels about Mary, Ælfric perfunctorily deals with the mysteries of the Virgin and is sensitive to Mary's limited role in scripture. Ælfric's homily, the "Assumptio Sanctae Mariae Virginis," warns that it is only heretics who spin stories about the Virgin, considered to be unorthodox by the church fathers.[67]

By contrast, the author of the *Meditations* places the affective aims of his narration above rigid adherence to the gospel text in presenting the pathetic poverty of Jesus' childhood: "These and other things about the boy Jesus you can contemplate. I have given you the occasion and you can enlarge on it (*extendas*) and follow it (*prosequaris*) as you please. Be a child with the child Jesus!"[68]

The author's choice of *prosequor* and *extendere* is both careful and revealing. In the medieval Latin lexicon *extendere* maintains its classical meaning "to extend."[69] Hence the author emphasizes addition to a

---

[64] Ibid., p. 34.

[65] Ibid., p. 35.

[66] Walsh, *Pre-Reformation English Spirituality*, p. 20.

[67] Ibid., p. 20.

[68] *Meditations on the Life of Christ*, trans. and ed. Ragusa and Green, p. 71. The Latin reads: "Haec et his similia de puero Jesu meditari potes; dedi tibi occasionem. Tu vero, sicut videbitur, extendas et prosequaris, sisque parvula cum parvulo Jesu." *Meditationes*, ed. Peltier, chap. 12, p. 526.

[69] Latham, *Revised Medieval Latin Word List*, s.v. *extensio*, p. 181.

present narrative structure, rather than the creation of a new one, which would imply the act of "fictionalizing" in our modern critical vocabulary. The etymological development of *prosequor* is somewhat more complex. While its classical meaning varied from "to attend" or "to accompany" to "to continue," in medieval Latin its general meaning was "to develop."[70] Both words suggest how tenuous was the distinction in such narratives between maintaining a factual premise for scriptural meditations and envisioning a consciously created scene.

Certainly Ælfric would have been distressed by the friar's depiction of the Nativity in the *Meditations*. In genuine joy the friar composes a scenario relating the excitement of the heavenly court at Christ's birth; angels virtually rain from the heavens, swiftly descending to see the Christ child. He conveys a sense of their angelic decorum and restrained anticipation, noting that they view the infant's face "in order of their rank."[71] He is doubtless conscious of his embellishment of Matthew but serenely remarks: "I think it pleasant to contemplate this scene of the angels, regardless of the truth of the matter."[72] "Truth" in this instance refers to the actuality of the historical event and clearly has little to do with the devotional merit of his meditation. What gives him spiritual pleasure is the harmonious sense of a divine order manifested in this regal celebration scene in the heavens. When the shepherds come to join in the adoration, recalling its source in Luke 2:15–21, its eschatological message is obvious: God incarnate mediates between heaven and earth, bringing a new order to all of humanity. The author conscientiously proceeds to interpret this scene for the Poor Clare, who may not glean this for herself.

[70] *OLD*, s.v. *Prosequor*, p. 1500. A number of the classical definitions of this verb are applicable when speaking of meditation, e.g., "to accompany," "to follow (with the eyes)," and "to accompany (a circumstance, action, with a particular reaction)." See also *Mediae latinitatis lexicon minus*, s.v. *prosequi*, p. 865. Here the verb is glossed in French as "developper," or "exposer." These are particularly applicable to visual meditation, the aim of which is to dramatically expound moral doctrine through dramatic interpolation, serving as a type of scriptural exegesis.

[71] *Meditations on the Life of Christ*, trans. and ed. Ragusa and Green, p. 38. The Latin reads: "Successive per ordines suos videre faciem Domini Dei sui." *Meditationes*, ed. Peltier, chap. 7, p. 520.

[72] *Meditations on the Life of Christ*, trans. and ed. Ragusa and Green, p. 38. The Latin reads: "Haec meditari de angelis jucundum puto, qualitercumque se habuerit veritas." *Meditationes*, ed. Peltier, chap. 7, p. 520.

41

This unabashed "fiction"-making puzzled early-twentieth-century scholars like George G. Coulton. It may seem curious that such a practice was encouraged by the friars, who were licensed to preach to simple people in an age of flourishing heresies. Coulton's view that the friars fed their sheep on "glosses and pious embroideries" or "sheer romance" is based on medieval criticism by Wyclif and others who shared his dislike of the mendicants.[73] In reply, however, David Jeffrey raises a perceptive point that must be examined further in light of the narrative movement of the *Meditations*. In Jeffrey's estimation Coulton ignores

> the key facet in Franciscan programs for making scripture available in the vernacular, which is in fact the use of extra materials to corroborate and strengthen the exegetical sense while at the same time providing a personalizing referent, thus sharpening the doctrinal point and purpose of all scriptural narrative.[74]

In Franciscan spirituality, scriptural meditation is a means of experiencing and internalizing truths. Bonaventure explains in the *Itinerarium* that "Sacred Scripture deals principally with the works of reparation."[75] Meditation on Christ's humanity is therefore the most efficacious means of preparing the heart for penance. Exegesis, or interpretation of scripture informed by external sources, has little merit by itself in Bonaventure's theology unless its outcome is penance. Accordingly, the penitent must accept the "whole law" of scripture, the

---

[73] George G. Coulton, *From St. Francis to Dante*, p. 303. Coulton notes that the friars did "little to spread the knowledge of of the actual text among the people, who were fed on glosses and pious embroideries rather than on the plain facts of Bible history. One of the most popular books of this kind, St. Bonaventura's *Hundred Meditations on the Life of Christ*, contains a good twenty per cent of glosses from the Fathers, or else of sheer romance, based upon the saint's own surmises of what might have happened . . . in spite of a general warning at the beginning of the book, and several others elsewhere, there is nothing in most cases to mark the transitions from Bible fact to pious fancy." On the contrary, the author, however unlike the learned Bonaventure he may be, is aware of the purpose of his narrative and as a conscientious religious instructor he is careful to make the distinctions that Coulton seems to have missed. See Jeffrey's response in *The Early English Lyric and Franciscan Spirituality*, pp. 47–49.

[74] Jeffrey, *The Early English Lyric*, p. 48.

[75] Bonaventure, *The Soul's Journey into God*, trans. and ed. Cousins, p. 91. The Latin reads: "Sacra enim Scriptura principaliter est de operibus reparationis." Bonaventure, *Itinerarium*, chap. 4, par. 5, p. 307.

chief moral message of Christ's life on earth, which is simply "these two commandments, the love of God and our neighbor."[76] Imitation is the final message of scripture interpreted by the Franciscans and implemented in Franciscan theology and devotion.

If the law is simply phrased, however, the need to imitate Christ is depicted as a simple task in the gospel harmonies. The author of the *Meditations* consciously creates an extraordinarily human Christ, sympathetically appealing to the reader's experience and spiritual condition as an incentive for confession. The result may seem comical or puzzling to the reader at times. The narrator's observations, for example, in chapter 15 on the omissions in the gospel are intriguing: "Or did the Lord remain idle so long and not do anything worthy of being remembered and recorded? If he did anything, why should it not be written like his other deeds? After all, this seems very strange."[77] He concludes that Christ, in his humility, desired to appear to his people like any other human being, a viator, leading a fairly unremarkable life before his ministry. Spiritual biography chronicles conversion, a growing intimacy with God, and acceptance of his will; the *Meditations* follows this pattern, making Christ the willing exemplar of all penitents. Therefore, little about his childhood matters besides those few incidents marking his special potential and grace. He worked, helped his parents, and, like most other good persons, seemed to the unredeemed of Israel to be simply a devout man without distinction. Christ's early portrait in the *Meditations* shows remarkable psychological insight, for its chief characteristic is a type of moderation, a private spirituality recognizable to all Christians: "He passed back and forth among men as though he did not notice anyone," seemingly engaged by the common cares of life like anyone else.[78] Since he had shown

---

[76] Bonaventure, *The Soul's Journey*, in *Works*, trans. and ed. Cousins, p. 91. The Latin reads: "Et Salvatur noster asserit; totam Legem Prophetasque pendere in duobis praeceptis eiusdem, scilicet dilectione Dei et proximi." Bonaventure, *Itinerarium*, chap. 4, par. 2, p. 307.

[77] *Meditations on the Life of Christ*, trans. and ed. Ragusa and Green, p. 94. The Latin reads: "Stetitne Dominus Jesus otiosis tanto temporem ut nihil faceret dignum recitatione et scriptura? Si enim fecisset, cur non fuisset scriptum, sicut reliqua facta sua? Omnino stupor videtur." *Meditationes*, ed. Peltier, chap. 15, p. 531.

[78] *Meditations on the Life of Christ*, trans. and ed. Ragusa and Green, p. 95. The Latin reads: "Pertransibat eundo et redeundo inter homines, ac si non viderit homines." *Meditationes*, ed. Peltier, chap. 15, p. 531.

unusual promise in his youth by teaching the elders in the temple, his community naturally waited for him to perform great deeds—a common phenomenon in all communities. To everyone's surprise and disgust, Jesus does "nothing to show any significance in prowess and valour."[79] The Franciscan imagines a chorus of angry relatives and disappointed neighbors, scoffing and prophesying Jesus' future: "He is a useless man, an idiot, a good for nothing, foolish, bad."[80]

The author admits that these imaginary events are not based in scripture but rather arise from the creative meditation proposed in the beginning of the work. However, the rationale behind his fictitious addition to the gospel story must be examined. In the early chapters of the *Meditations*, the Franciscan author intentionally portrays Christ as humbly assuming the guise of Everyman; as in all other spiritual biography, Christ's acceptance of his mission assumes the nature of conversion for the benefit of sinners, at which point he willfully departs from an average life. The author intensifies Christ's human nature, even exaggerates in these chapters, to prepare the reader for the emotional shock necessary for repentance when he or she experiences the Passion with Christ in the latter third of the work. By juxtaposing ordinary human history with the ministry and subsequent Passion, the author subtly discloses the theologically complex and solemn truth of the Passion: Christ remained a simple man in many ways throughout his ministry, yet he willingly chose the Crucifixion.

Devotions based on Christ's life as exemplified in the *Meditations* thus become a series of startling revelations about Christ's human nature and suffering. The meditator imaginatively accompanies Christ through the mundane experiences of his youth, through the slow process of temptation, illumination, and conversion, to confront the grace-infused Savior of the Crucifixion. The temporal framework of the narrative, lengthened considerably to include the homeliest details, reminds the reader that the compression of the gospel stories veils the

---

[79] *Meditations on the Life of Christ*, trans. and ed. Ragusa and Green, p. 95. The Latin reads: "Nulla opera faciebat . . . speciem aliquam probitatis et virilitatis." *Meditationes*, ed. Peltier, chap. 15, p. 531.

[80] *Meditations on the Life of Christ*, trans. and ed. Ragusa and Green, p. 95. The Latin reads: "Iste est quidam inutilis, ipse est idiota et homo de nihil et stultus et insipiens!" *Meditationes*, ed. Peltier, chap. 15, p. 531.

tedium, the humdrum aspect of the human nature Christ adopted. Nonetheless, this is the reality of the penitent's life; penance belongs not to the realm of the heroic but to the domain of daily human experience with its less sensational temptations.

Our experience with the Passion lyrics should remind us that the focus on Christ's humanity does not diffuse but intensifies his divinity. Franciscanism celebrates this "coincidence of opposites," or Christ's role as mediator between divinity and the created world. [81] While Bonaventure expresses his own understanding of this miracle in chapter 6 of the *Itinerarium* in the language of speculative theology, the common expression of this wonder is translated in those very details of the gospel harmonies that puzzle modern readers. In the thirteenth century the Franciscan monk wondered what the angels brought Christ to eat after he had fasted forty days: "The angels said to him, 'Lord, you have fasted long. What do you wish us to prepare for you?' And He said, 'Go to my beloved mother. If she has something at hand, let her send it, for I eat no food as gladly as hers.'" [82]

This fictitious detail, while it is clearly a fanciful addition to any account of Christ's life, acknowledges that part of Christ's nature which admitted human affections and also, like the penitent, struggled with sin and willfulness. This kind of narrative addition provided comfort and incentive for the penitent, who realized that Christ truly understands fallen humanity. Such details are the "personalizing referent" of which David Jeffrey speaks. [83] In addition, appeals to everyday life reminded the reader or listener of the incarnational element of Christianity that infuses ordinary objects and places with a sacramental meaning.

As James Olney points out, however, in *Forms of Autobiography*, "Meaning emerges with our perception of a pattern, and there can be no pattern in chronologically or geographically discrete items and

[81] Ewert H. Cousins, "The Coincidence of Opposites in the Christology of St. Bonaventure," *EFran* 18 (1968): 15–31.

[82] *Meditations on the Life of Christ*, trans. and ed. Ragusa and Green, p. 125. The Latin reads: "Dicunt ei angeli: Domine, multum jejunastis, quid vultis ut vobis paremus? Et ille: Ite ad matrem meam charissimam, et si quid habet ad manus, deferte; quia de nullis cibis sic libenter vescor, sicut de suis." *Meditationes*, ed. Peltier, chap. 17, p. 540.

[83] Jeffrey, *The Early English Lyric*, p. 48.

elements."[84] Like the pilgrimage, a selectively ordered journey with an immanent spiritual destination, or a sacrament that orders and sanctifies otherwise meaningless gestures, the *Meditations* provides the reader with an overlying metaphor or form for meditative experience. The metaphor, Christ's life, makes historical and spiritual connections between events, creating a design corresponding to the meditator's own life. The author of the *Meditations* is conscious of this pattern and how its experiential nature functions with "biography," or the external life of the penitent, as a process of self-knowledge and spiritual revelation.

Colin Morris attributes the development of biography to the Cistercians in his study of individualism in Western culture; for Bernard, biography was indeed "the confession of God's goodness and the writer's sin," or a process of self-awareness ultimately leading to penance and conversion in the Augustinian tradition.[85] Caroline W. Bynum, in turn, has rightly questioned the use of the term "individual" in relation to the potent personal expressions of spirituality in twelfth- and thirteenth-century religious texts.[86] She explains that what Bernard, Abelard, and others discovered was not a singular religious path, or individuality, but "'the soul' (anima), or 'self' (seipsum), or the 'inner man' (homo interior). And this self, this inner landscape on which they laid fresh and creative emphasis, was not what we mean by 'the individual.'"[87] What the Cistercians discovered, Bynum maintains, was not biography but spiritual autobiography.

Unlike biography or autobiography, which relies on the external facts of chronology, physical landscapes, and empirical causality for its authority, spiritual autobiography draws its authority from an eternal pattern of conversion.[88] Medieval devotion thus imposes a collective scheme on all spiritual growth that disregards the external facts that make their claim to individuality. As Ira Bruce Nadel observes in *Biography: Fiction, Fact, and Form*, the various genres of medieval

---

[84] Olney, *Forms of Autobiography*, p. 31.

[85] Colin Morris, *The Discovery of the Individual*, p. 161.

[86] Caroline Walker Bynum, *Jesus as Mother: Studies in the Spirituality of the High Middle Ages*. See chap. 3, "Did the Twelfth Century Discover the Individual?" pp. 82–109.

[87] Ibid., p. 87.

[88] Ira Bruce Nadel, *Biography: Fiction, Fact, and Form*, p. 2.

spiritual literature—legend, hagiography, and spiritual autobiography—are dominant when individual experience is secondary in importance to a collective spiritual tradition.[89]

How are we then to explain the instruction to the penitent in Franciscan meditation to seek an individual spiritual experience—more specifically, an experience which is self-created and yet contains moral instruction that leads to the "truth" of *imitatio* in everyday life? Concerned with the development of the concept of fiction in Renaissance literature, William Nelson addressed only one facet of the problem of truthfulness in medieval spiritual narratives:

> The unquestionable verity of Biblical story relegated all other histories to the realm of human uncertainty, so that a very large body of apocryphal, hagiographical, and quasi-historical narrative, if not demonstrably false or harmful to the soul, could be tolerated as perhaps true.[90]

As we have seen, the Franciscan author of the *Meditations* is sensitive to these very questions about the orthodoxy of imagined and embellished scriptural meditations. Yet his first concern is to enable a penitent, the Poor Clare for whom he wrote the *Meditations*, to internalize the truth of scripture to such a degree that she might go forth and live like Christ, whatever her vocation. With this aim in mind, the Franciscan author of the *Meditations* systematizes his work to ensure that this pattern is imposed on the narrator's own life, integrating the biblical narrative of Christ's life with the penitent's. He divides his chapters chronologically, making the entire work a week's meditation, to be repeated each week.[91] The Poor Clare was to read the nativity sections on Monday and progress chronologically toward the Passion,

[89] Ibid., p. 6.

[90] William Nelson, *Fact or Fiction: The Dilemma of the Renaissance Storyteller*, p. 35.

[91] *Meditationes*, ed. Peltier, chap. 100, p. 629. The author explains: "Meditationes vero sic divide, ut die Lunae incipiens, procurras usque ad apertionem libri in synagoga; die Mercurii exinde, usque in miniserium Mariae et Marthae; die Jovis abinde, usque ad passionem; die veneris et Sabbati, usque ad resurrectionem; die vero Dominica, ipsam resurrectionem, et usque in finem; et sic per singulas hebdomadas facias; ut ipsa meditationes tibi reddas familiares: quod quanto magis facies, tanto facilius tibi occurrent, atque jucundius. Libenter converseris cum Domino Jesu, et vitam ipsius tanquam Evangelium, ad imitationem beatae Caeciliae, in corde studeas insepapraviliter collocare."

which she read commemoratively on Friday. Naturally she read the Resurrection sections on Sunday. She thus witnessed Christ's life weekly, inextricably meshing her life with the gospel in an internal rhythm like that of the liturgical year but even more personal. Through meditation she participated vicariously in Christian history, achieving a type of *imitatio*. The Gospels become a mirror, according to the *Meditations*, into which the penitent gazes for a clearer view of his or her soul's progress.

This incorporeal landscape, embellished by the individual's imagination, offered the layperson a vision of the incarnational world that Francis himself inhabited. John Fleming notes that the "Franciscan literary style, like the Franciscan conception of religious life, attempts to reestablish in a flesh and blood world a vibrant realization of the transcendent."[92] The increasing number of mystics and visionaries in fourteenth-century England indicates a hunger in late-medieval society for temporal spiritual experiences, or individual confirmation of the spirit and a divine order in a chaotic world on the brink of religious reformation. Through *imitatio* Francis promised to initiate the individual into an elect body of believers who could experience intensely this transcendent world. This is basically what the cult of monasticism proffered the elect of the early-medieval period through ritual and the *vita contemplativa*. The Franciscans offered conversion, an awakening of the human spirit to a higher reality, to all Catholics inclusively.

Francis's life served as an example of this slow awakening to a divine presence in everyday life. Perhaps more important, the Franciscans conceived of Christ's own life in these very human terms, making conformity to his life a possibility for the common believer, while not diminishing the mysteries of the Crucifixion. Spiritual biography, like Franciscan meditation, affirms the purpose of Christian life by celebrating a "salvational pattern evident in human history."[93] While Franciscan meditation creates an interior landscape in which to explore imaginatively the role of the individual in this eschatological framework, spiritual biography outwardly manifests this role in action.

It hardly seems coincidental that the gospel harmonies, simplified

---

[92] Fleming, *An Introduction to the Franciscan Literature*, p. 250.
[93] Carruthers, "Time, Apocalypse, and the Plot of *Piers Plowman*," p. 177.

versions of Christ's life that served a meditative purpose, became popular at the same time that English literature became marked by a preoccupation with private religious experience, as in *Pearl*, *Piers Plowman*, *The Book of Margery Kempe*, Richard Rolle's *Incendium amoris*, and Julian of Norwich's *Divine Showings*. None of these works was composed by members of a specific religious order; like Francis, their authors acknowledge the importance of the church's guidance, but each maintains spiritual independence by depicting unique paths of expression. Each stresses vision as a means of coming to know God. To what types of devotional literature were such writers and less educated audiences exposed in order to learn participatory meditation?

Elizabeth Salter and Margaret Deanesly have completed detailed investigations on the most common English translations of the *Meditations* and its manuscript tradition.[94] Above all else, their discoveries imply a firmly rooted tradition of lay meditation in England. Nicholas Love's edition of 1415, *Myrrour of the Blessed Lyf of Jesu Christ*, was the most widely read book of the fifteenth century.[95] It was printed by Caxton in 1488(?) and by Wynkyn de Worde in 1517 and 1523, indicating that both aristocratic and bourgeois laymen were exposed to Franciscan meditation in the Bonaventuran tradition.[96] Salter, however, insists that "Love presupposes a certain knowledge of such processes in his readers" and suggests that imaginative meditation was an integral part of penitential devotions long before the literacy rate rose in England.[97]

According to Deanesly, gospel harmonies like the *Meditations* in its various forms provided for most people the only alternative to reading scripture or listening to the unintelligible Latin. Direct access to the Gospels was prohibited to the laity by the Council of Toulouse in 1229—a decision confirmed in England in 1408 by Archbishop Arundel, who later approved the production of Love's text.[98] The

[94] Salter, *Nicholas Love's* Myrrour; Margaret Deanesly, "The Gospel Harmony of John de Caulibus, or St. Bonaventure," pp. 10–19.

[95] Deanesly, "The Gospel Harmony of John de Caulibus, or St. Bonaventure," p. 19.

[96] Deanesly, "Vernacular Books in England in the Fourteenth and Fifteenth Centuries," pp. 349–58.

[97] Salter, *Nicholas Love's* Myrrour, p. 167.

[98] Margaret Deanesly, *The Lollard Bible*, pp. 36, 321.

gospel harmonies were acceptable because they served a carefully defined devotional purpose and were unlikely to be misinterpreted or misconstrued. They did not claim to be substitutes for the "Word" itself, which remained powerfully in the possession of the clergy.

Although Love was a Carthusian, Salter insists that his translation of the work gives further emphasis to the characteristically Franciscan elements of the original; Love "moves in harmony with the unknown Franciscan."[99] The number of translations of the *Meditations*, as well as its wide audience, implies that the common man or woman of thirteenth-, fourteenth-, and fifteenth-century England received a uniquely Franciscan version of the Gospels, with its emphasis on the Passion, realistic detail, and firsthand experience of events. Even Sir Thomas More, who became the champion of conservative Catholicism, advises the common people to avoid heresy by reading and practicing meditations in "Bonaventure of the Lyf of Christ," clearly referring to the *Meditationes* in one manifestation or another.[100] For those laypersons who could not read, meditation was taught orally, as in the *Meditations on the Supper of Our Lord*.

The *Meditations on the Supper of Our Lord*, dated roughly 1315–30, provides an interesting perspective on the way in which Franciscan meditation was taught to an illiterate laity. It also reveals how such meditative narratives dramatically conveyed their penitential function to believers with little or no knowledge of Catholic dogma. The connection with the Franciscans is so evident that the manuscript's early editors unquestioningly attributed it to Bonaventure; indeed, the *Supper* is a fairly close translation of the *Meditations* in octosyllabic couplets. The lyrical quality of the work indicates that the English language was a far more flexible tool for religious expression before Rolle's mystical works than is commonly believed. The *Supper* is compiled in Harley manuscript 1701, which contains the popular penitential work *Handlyng Synne*. The purpose of the *Supper* is clear. The invocation in the Prologue to "save all the congrecacyon" suggests that the text was read or recited aloud to an audience, presumably of all

---

[99] Salter, *Nicholas Love's* Myrrour, p. 320.

[100] Roger Lovatt, "The Imitation of Christ in Late Medieval England," *Transactions of the Royal Historical Society*, 5th ser., vol. 18, p. 97.

estates, since it continues with the request that each "man in hys degre" respond with an "amen."[101] Like its source, the text is specifically evangelical and affective, asking each listener to "opene þyn herte," as would any prayer meeting today. From the very beginning this work establishes the spiritual strength that imaginative re-creation of the Gospels gives to the devout, confirming the Franciscan emphasis on the efficacy of vision: "Whan þou þenkest þys yn þy þoȝt / Thyr may no fende noye þe with noȝt" (p. 2, lines 21–22).

In keeping with the Franciscan meditative tradition, the *Supper* imaginatively transforms the penitent into a companion of Christ, each act the Lord performs ritually called to memory. Unlike the *Meditations*, however, the *Supper* has been edited for public use rather than for the private contemplative; hence the author's repeated instructions to "beholde" and "þenk" or recall iconographic images. He is particularly concerned with creating a vivid historical scene; he urges his audience to think of the Last Supper as an actual occurrence, a dramatic event with witnesses, as related in "Seynt Martyals legende" (p. 3, line 51). The author employs the dramatic device of conjuring ocular proof as evidence that "þys soper was real." He claims that the table on which the Last Supper was celebrated is "at rome men have seyn, / yn Seynt Johne Chyrche þe latereyn" (p. 3, lines 73–74). The friar's sermons were famous, or infamous, for their use of ocular proof, personal experience, and colorful exempla.

An examination of the narrative suggests a close relationship between such dramatic, meditative texts and the developing cycle dramas that flourished when the *Meditations* was most popular in the fifteenth century. After the Prologue to the *Supper* the narrative voice diminishes as the scenes are dramatically disclosed, and it is eventually absorbed entirely in the dialogue itself. As in all other Franciscan narrative that stresses experience, the distance between teller and listener, spiritual director and meditator, dissolves to enable the latter to participate fully in the scene. The betrayal scene is a good example of this subtle and intentional merger of voices to engross the audience in the actual event taking place before its eyes (p. 4, lines 97–102):

---

[101] *Meditations on the Supper of Our Lord*, ed. J. Meadows Cowper, p. 1, line 8. All further quotations from this work are taken from this edition.

> Byholde now, man, what sorowe and wo
> þy dycyplys toke to hem þo;
> Þys voys as a swerd here hertes persed,
> And to ete anone þey seced.
> Eche loked on ouþer with grysly ye,
> and seyd, "lorde wheþer it by y?"

At this dramatic moment the meditator gazes upon the disciples, who gaze upon each other, equally intent on discerning the traitor. Of course, Judas continues to eat as if nothing has happened (p. 4, lines 105–108):

> Pryuyly þan Jon to cryst gan prey,
> And seyd, "lorde, who shal þe betrey?
> For specyal love cryst hyt hym tolde,
> "Iudas skaryot," he seyd, "beholde."

The listener or meditator thus narrows his or her focus from the general picture to the particular detail of Judas's face; directed by Jesus, he or she, as though a disciple, enters the dramatic movement of the scene. Rhythm and repetition culminate in this final command to see, which comes no longer from the narrator but from Christ himself. This experiential movement might be compared to the attention to detail that Rosalie Greene and Isa Ragusa find characteristic of the illustrations in Franciscan manuscripts. The vivid re-creation of scenes results in a sequential narrative effect, thus drawing the meditator into the action instead of asking him or her to view it objectively.

Meditations on the Supper of Our Lord is primarily concerned with the purgative stage of spiritual development. In this light one of the most interesting and significant additions to both texts is the penitential scene that follows the deposition of Jesus's body in the tomb. The attention given to this event in both manuscripts reflects its importance; thematically this depiction of the first "confession" of the new church, enacted by the Virgin and the disciples, exemplifies and grants a powerful authority to the Franciscan mission.

In both works, after the deposition Mary retreats to the home of Joseph of Arimathea with Mary Magdalene and John. The Virgin laments, and her *planctus* do not cease until Peter arrives with the rest of the disciples. They, however, have far greater need to mourn, having deserted Jesus in his hour of need. They are remorseful and initially want information about the Crucifixion; their plight is parallel to every believer's, for not only have they been sinful and submerged their love for Christ in a well of human fear, but they feel compelled to witness or see the Crucifixion for themselves: "Þey asked þe doyng of here dere lorde, / Jon tolde hem þe processe every aworde" (p. 34, lines 1079–80).

Appropriately, there is a great deal of weeping and self-recrimination, until the Virgin assures them that the Crucifixion is part of a divine plan, one that includes the remission of sin. The scene directly alludes to the sacrament of penance, and Mary's next speech explains the role of affective devotion therein: the disciples "here confessyun / Maden and weptyn with lamentacyun" (p. 34, lines 1085 –86). In this way the *Supper* confirms the correct response to descriptions of the Passion that abound in Franciscan penitential literature and the necessity of compunction of heart that enables the ever-wayward human will to conform to Christ. Mary's speech takes the form of absolution (p. 34, lines 1103–1106):

> 3e weten weyl how benygne my dere sone was,
> Ly3tly to for3yve al maner of trespas;
> Douteþ 3e no þyng of hys grete mercy,
> For largely he 3yfþ þat cryeþ hyt hertly.

The scene successfully illustrates the manner in which confession strengthens faith in the church, as well as the freedom with which the Passion story might be told to emphasize the purpose of affective devotion. It is important to recognize the Franciscan nature of such dramatic presentation: like Franciscan sermons, which vividly convey truth through exempla or stories, the *Meditations* and the *Supper* consciously teach by the creation of experiences, rather than through a purely homiletic process.

In the *Meditations*, Christ's painful moment of surrender in the Garden of Gethsemane, in which he fully accepts the will of his Father, is followed by an explanation of the four wills of Christ—a doctrinal exposition clearly not intended for a popular audience. In the *Meditations on the Supper of Our Lord* the author translates this penitential and theologically Franciscan emphasis on perfect conformity to Christ into a dramatic scene that focuses on the importance of a joyful

53

acceptance of his will. Christ, having acknowledged the element of resistance in his human nature to pain and death, responds lyrically to his role, with an eloquent exposition of his motives (p. 13, lines 391–96):

> Þan cryst answered, wyth mylde state:
> Soules salvatyun y wyl algate,
> Þarfore to dey raþer y chese,
> Þan we þe soules yn helle shulde lese,
> Þy whych my fader formed to his lykenes:
> Hys wyl be ydo, y wyll no lesse.

Franciscan meditative texts taught the laity, in addition to the fundamental importance of penance in the scheme of salvation, that envisioning and imaginative participation provided an affective experience comparable to that of the disciples, or of Francis himself. *Imitatio* could be achieved by all Christians, regardless of their economic, gender, or lay status. Many of these texts have yet to be examined, but such explorations promise to be fruitful and will certainly enrich our conception of medieval lay society. Literary historians, in particular, cannot afford to ignore the fact that laypersons were embellishing scripture, creating narratives in their private devotions, long before they actually learned to express themselves on the written page. The idea is provocative and justifies broadening our canon to include the devotional works that may have nurtured the seeds of poems like *Pearl* and *Piers Plowman*.

Joseph and Mary in Bethlehem, MS Douce 219, fol. 115ʳ, by permission of the Bodleian Library, Oxford University.

3

Re-visioning in
The Book of Margery Kempe

In the *Fioretti*, the legends of Francis and his followers, the dusty roads, dry fields and treacherous steeps of Umbria become a dramatic sphere of vision and miracle. The frequency of supernatural events in Franciscan legends suggests a heightened awareness of God's presence in the tangible world; this "exemplarism," so basic in Francis's own spirituality, eventually found expression in Bonaventure's theological program of ascent, which recognized the importance of vision and sense experience in coming to a knowledge of God.

Francis's Italy, surely not through coincidence, abounded with cults devoted to holy women of vision, among whom his spiritual protégée, Clare, is perhaps best known to us today. Her prominence in the cult of medieval saints is clearly linked to Francis's own popularity. The lives of those women saints who were less fortunately circumstanced, however, or unassociated with the founder of a particular male order, have disappeared from our records until recently. Seeking to reestablish the feminine religious voice, Elizabeth Petroff has translated the curious life of Blessed Ghirardesca of Pisa, whose confessor recorded her history around 1269, when the second generation of the Franciscan order established itself under Bonaventure.[1] Her life is of particular interest because, although Ghirardesca was enclosed in a convent, she shared with Margery Kempe a spiritual vocabulary and similar sense of burgeoning identity. In spite of their very different vocations, both envisioned their roles in eschatological history in private and social terms. The lives of both women are also characterized by a Franciscan Christocentrism, with its emphasis on the incarnational and the providential direction of scripture. More important, both fulfilled their potential as loving human beings with guidance sought and affirmed through participating in scenes of the Gospels or pseudo-biblical visions.

Ghirardesca's richly woven tale of conversion and vision is preserved in a manuscript in a monastery in Pisa. But preservation often means silence in relation to women's narratives; certainly Margery Kempe's *Book* shared the mixed blessing of preservation with numerous neglected saints' lives. The saints' lives that Petroff has skillfully spun out for modern scholars are also similar to Margery's *Book* in that they are strangely textured, exotic, and equally erotic tales of conversion and mystical vision; like some of Margery's visions and meditations in the *Book*, they evoke myth and poetic dream vision, as do *Pearl* and *Piers Plowman*, in their symbol-laden, sometimes fragmented narratives.

Blessed Ghirardesca's story is a familiar medieval tale of marriage and self-discovery. Like Margery, Ghirardesca must "admonish" her husband to retreat from his worldly existence with her.[2] For her, as for many other women of her day, enclosure provided a spiritual freedom in which she found inexpressible joy.[3] She also developed powers of mystical vision and was consulted by the friars, who sought her "signs and prodigies."[4] Once, on the Feast Day of the Blessed Virgin, as Ghirardesca prayed and listened to the Franciscan choir sing, she had a vision:

> At the point when the choir of the Franciscans was singing, Holy, Holy, Holy, three rays of sun came through the window next to the altar, and three doves, and likewise

[1] For background on visionary activity as spiritual authority in the lives of thirteenth-century women saints see Elizabeth Petroff, *Consolation of the Blessed*, chap. 1, "Saints and Saint's Lives: The Paradox for Women," pp. 1–13. Also see Carolly Erikson, *The Medieval Vision*, chap. 8, "The Wisdom of Women," pp. 181–212.

[2] Petroff, *Consolation of the Blessed*, p. 121.

[3] Ibid., p. 87.

[4] Ibid., p. 97.

three golden stars. Two of the doves were of a hyacinth color; they perched on the right and left shoulder of the priest, who was performing the mysteries of the Mass at the altar and supported his arms. At the altar, a third dove, white as snow, raised up the body of the Lord, just in front of the priest's hands, so that the priest, believing he was touching the host, invisibly stroked the dove—which the holy woman saw openly.[5]

Her vision is richly sensuous and symbolic. On one level of inter-pretation it clearly speaks of the trinitarian nature of God, which is the root of Ghirardesca's faith; it alludes to the way in which the sacramen-tal bread miraculously transforms into flesh, the fluttering dove, dur-ing the ritual of the Eucharist. Yet to analyze this vision as we would an allegory is to impose limitations on it, and understanding it is as elusive a process as interpreting the luminous symbolism of the Middle En-glish *Pearl*. In many medieval religious works truth is veiled in poetic language of ritual and vision, creating for the reader a literature of individual experience. Confronted with uncertainties and ambiguities in our reading of spiritual experience, however, we mistakenly seek definitions. We ask ourselves whether Ghirardesca had a corporeal vision or saw the sunlight and created an elaborate metaphor for the Eucharist, thus experiencing an "intellectual vision" as defined by Augustine.[6]

Carolly Erikson astutely notes that our problem with reading medi-eval literature is perceptual, and I would illustrate this by pointing to the spiritual experiences of women who do not formulate their visions in conceptually acceptable, hierarchical patterns provided by trained intellects:

> Our lexicon associates visions with mysticism, irrationality, occultism, imprac-ticality, and madness. From our point of view, the visionary is a person who sees what isn't there; his [her] visions separate him [her] from reality. In the Middle Ages, visions defined reality.[7]

According to the definition of the Catholic church, Margery was not a saint. Yet she was a visionary, like Ghirardesca, of startlingly similar power:

---

[5] Ibid.
[6] Erikson, *The Medieval Vision*, p. 37.
[7] Ibid., p. 30.

> On a day as þis creatur was heryng hir Messe, a ȝong man and a good prest heldyng up the Sacrament in hys handys ouyr hys hed, þe Sacrament schok and flekeryd to and fro as a dowe flekeryth wyth hir wengys. &, whan he held up þe chalys wyth þe precyows sacrament, þe chalys mevyd to & fro as it xuld a fallyn owt of hys handys.[8]

Unless we deny Margery's credibility altogether—and some of the most powerful men and women of her day did not—we must accept the fact that she possessed powers of vision generally outside our everyday experience. To modern empirical thinkers, imbued with a sense of corporeality, the visual imagination is the realm of childish fantasy, of "fiction" that delineates truth and untruth, the real and the make-believe in irrevocable boundaries. As Erikson states, however, medieval people perceived the world differently: "Their sight was different from ours in kind; accepting a more inclusive concept of reality, they saw more than we do."[9]

Discovered by Colonel Butler-Bowden in 1934, *The Book of Margery Kempe* has proven to be as controversial as Margery herself was after her religious conversion. Margery Kempe was born into a family of economic and political prominence in Bishop's Lynn, Norfolk, circa 1373. Like most medieval women, little is known of her life before her marriage to John Kempe in 1393, with whom she bore fourteen children. Although her autobiography is a powerful social document in many respects, readers who wish to flesh out the middle class woman's everyday existence will be disappointed. *The Book of Margery Kempe*, recorded in two parts by two different scribes and completed in 1438, chronicles the singular religious vocation this late medieval laywoman shaped for herself despite social, cultural, and religious opposition.

In her *Book*, Margery explains how a vision of Christ initiated her conversion from a despairing, materialistic sinner into an empowered exemplar of the Christian life of prayer and service. Incorporating elements from hagiography, gospel harmonies, and mystical treatises, Margery's *Book* is a peculiar, hybrid creation, vividly describing her domestic and foreign pilgrimages, as well as her courageous efforts to teach reformation in England through an orthodox revival of the apostolic ideal.

[8] Kempe, *The Book of Margery Kempe*, p. 47.
[9] Erikson, *The Medieval Vision*, p. 29.

As Maureen Fries has explained in her seminal discussion of Margery Kempe's *Book* and critics, Margery's life followed the threefold pattern of mystical life. Nonetheless, her status as a married laywoman, her explicit challenges to male authority, and her demonstrative spirituality, so un-English in its public expression, baffled not only her contemporaries, but modern readers as well.

The shockingly slow acceptance of Margery's *Book*, which should have been one of the most provocative discoveries of our century for historians and literary scholars, suggests a rather suspicious view of medieval ontology that must be revised if we are to understand lay devotion in the thirteenth century and, for our limited purposes here, the attraction the Franciscan movement held for laypersons. Not only did Francis rely on visions and dreams for spiritual guidance, but Franciscan devotional exercises actively developed the visual imagination, requiring the layperson to extemporize visions and then find solace and affirmation in these consciously embellished scenes of Christ's life. Unless we accept vision as a potent source of spiritual growth and authority, many of the medieval visionary works that, like Margery's, do not conform to Augustine's schematic breakdown of visions lose their validity.

Margery Kempe's *Book* has suffered this fate. Her strong personality and her formidable resistance to definition baffled her peers as well as modern scholars. She has been called both a "mystic" and an "apprentice saint."[10] Her powerful, orally derived knowledge of scripture drew her into the dangerous circle of Lollards in her society. Examined in the equally narrow context of modern psychology, Margery has been assigned a similarly peripheral role as an eccentric by many contemporary readers.[11] Even Hope Emily Allen, who introduced *The Book of Margery Kempe* into our historical and literary canon, considered Margery "neurotic," "physically and nervously overstrained."[12] Allen

[10] See Louise Collis, *The Apprentice Saint*. Also see Roland Maissoneve, "Margery Kempe and the Eastern and Western Tradition of the 'Perfect Fool,'" in Marion Glasscoe, ed., *The Medieval Mystical Tradition in England*, Papers Read at Dartington Hall, July, 1982, p. 1.

[11] Donald R. Howard, *Writers and Pilgrims: Medieval Pilgrim Narratives and Their Posterity*, p. 25. Howard views Kempe as an eccentric and singular religious phenomenon rather than as a central figure in the lay devotional movement.

[12] Kempe, *the Book of Margery Kempe*, p. lxiv.

elicited "an expert judgement on Margery's neuroticism" from Herbert Thurston, who applied his experience with "psychological types like Margery" and found that she had that mysterious, peculiarly feminine disease "hysteria."[13] All of the above testifies not only to our modern critical inadequacies but also to the self-imposed limitations of the human intellect shaped by a learning that excludes all but the readily definable.

How, then, should we read *The Book of Margery Kempe*? As social history, Margery's *Book* is an invaluable source of political, social, and cultural information that we cannot afford to ignore. Her autobiography is one of the major extant texts vividly illustrating the spiritual concerns of a middle-class laywoman in the fifteenth century. For the literary historian Margery's memoirs indicate that various modes of experience, including vision and sacramental ritual, provided the clearest route to the medieval layperson's self-knowledge; religious vision was the medieval "corollary" to a "continually deepening relationship with the divine."[14] This chapter examines one realm of her visionary activity — imaginative meditation — which she practiced as a devotional exercise in preparation for prayer and penance.[15] Such devotional exercises encouraged Margery to probe her private response to spiritual truths and the various duties the church assigned to her as a laywoman. For Margery imaginative meditation became a vital process of self-revelation, and she naturally included several long sequences of meditation in her spiritual autobiography.

Margery's meditations exhibit a deepening sense of her spiritual potential and the role she must choose to manifest God's transforming power to the world. Her *Book* chronicles her constancy in the face of external turmoil and persecution. Her meditations on Christ's life and humanity, in turn, form a reflective commentary on the process of her spiritual maturation. Margery's "fictional" envisionings of scriptural scenes emerge from or respond to her deepest anxieties about her own and others' salvation. Ultimately they confirm her conversion by eliciting and celebrating the boundless compassion that gave Margery the

---

[13] Ibid., p. lxv.

[14] Petroff, *Consolation of the Blessed*, p. 77.

[15] Martin Thornton, *Margery Kempe: An Example in the English Pastoral Tradition*, p. 43.

courage to serve Christ joyfully in "þis wretchyd world" from which she once "coueyted gretly to be delyueryd" (p. 20, lines 7–8). In an early meditation Christ specifically commands Margery to "abyden & languren in lofe" (p. 20, lines 8–9). Through her powerful visions of Christ's suffering, Margery internalizes "þe wey of hy perfeccyon, whech parfyth wey Cryst ower Savyowr in hys propyr persoone examplyd" (p. 2, lines 2–4). Margery's imaginative experiences assured her that her unconventional vocation of service and prayer had an authority in scripture above social custom or ideology.

In turn, Margery's imitation of Christ led to a deeper understanding of scripture, giving her the power and authority to teach others, not from a formal, and thus prohibited, learning but from experience. Like the unlearned Francis, who Bonaventure tells us became "filled with knowledge," Margery also acquired a spiritual learning enabling her to explain "doubtful questions" and bring "hidden things to light."[16] While the Lollard heresy of Margery's day gave her forthright observations about clerical corruption and her application of scripture to contemporary problems dangerous implications, the spirit of her teaching was Franciscan and orthodox in its origins. Bonaventure, in defending the mysterious source of Francis's own wisdom, states:

> Nor should it sound odd that the holy man should have received from God an understanding of the Scriptures, since through his perfect imitation of Christ he carried into practice the truths described in them, and, through the abundant anointing of the Holy Spirit, had their Teacher within himself in his heart.[17]

As Clarissa Atkinson indicates in her study of Margery Kempe, it is impossible to divorce Margery's spirituality and its forms of expression from Franciscan devotion: "The Franciscan ethos and pathos color almost every aspect of the piety of Margery Kempe, from her love of sermons to the meditations that focused on homely details of the Nativity and Passion."[18]

---

[16] Bonaventure, *Legenda S. Francisci*, chap. 11, par. 2, p. 536.

[17] Ibid. The Latin reads: "Nec absonum, si vir sanctus Scripturarum a Deo intellectum acceperat, cum per imitationem Christi perfectam veritatem ipsarum descriptam gestaret in opere et per sancti spiritus unctionem plenariam doctorem earum apud se haberet in corde."

[18] Clarissa Atkinson, *Mystic and Pilgrim: The Book and the World of Margery Kempe*, p. 139.

Margery voices concern about the inaccuracy of her *Book*'s temporal framework and her adamant desire to record nothing "but þat sche knew rygth wel for very trewth" (p. 5, lines 18–19). Her inclusion of meditations and personally embellished renditions of scriptural scenes concurs with the Franciscan view that the "the literal story was less important than the penitence it produced; any incident that moved the believer was 'true' in the sense that mattered."[19] Modern readers of Margery's *Book* need to consider the complex role of the visual imagination in her private spiritual development and regard her "fiction making" in the greater context of Franciscan-influenced religious expression.

Clearly we are right to be startled by the similarities between Ghirardesca's eucharistic vision and Margery's curious experience more than two hundred years later. While they share an iconography or symbol system, the authority that the visions lend to both women in their respective worlds is the most important likeness. Ghirardesca silently muses upon her vision until she decides to share it with the Friars Minor.[20] She then serves as a witness of nondiscursive truths that, rather than indicating hysteria or an overactive imagination, are considered the privilege of a special sanctity.

Margery's visions also enable her to witness God's power to her spiritual community. Like many saints, she serves on occasion as a prophet or "seer"; this eucharistic vision betokened "an erdene," an earthquake (p. 47, line 30). Neither vision, however, is the subject of speculative discussion on the nature of the Trinity or the Eucharist. It is fair to say that Julian of Norwich's "shewing" of a knowledge of speculative theology, as much as the pathos of her vision, has impressed scholars like Edmund Colledge and David Knowles, who equate her with the male mystics.[21] Unlike purely experiential or meditative visions, Julian's are intellectual, clarifying dogmatic concepts for which we naturally lack evidence.

Margery and Ghirardesca's nonspeculative visions, however, enabled both women to step outside their roles as women, deprived of au-

---

[19] Ibid., p. 139.

[20] Petroff, *Consolation of the Blessed*, p. 96.

[21] See David Knowles, *The English Mystical Tradition*; and E. Colledge, *The Medieval Mystics in England*.

thoritative voices by their sexual status and lack of education. And visions gave all three women a "public language' and a visible office in the world, in spite of their positions as women in their respective cultures.[22] In the Middle Ages visions became a medium of exploration for women in multiple, coexistent realms of experience — emotional, spiritual, sexual; they gave women the imaginative space to question and defy spiritual truths that cenobitic monasticism clothed in terms hostile to woman's very existence. The fluctuating, uncertain world in which they lived, often as both despised and "exemplary" figures, intensifying their own sense of sin and inadequacy, needed to be explained somehow.

To accept her *Book* on its own terms and thus understand it, we must first acknowledge that Margery's epistemology is necessarily subjective. As a largely uneducated layperson, at least until she could cajole a priest into reading to her, her world and her perception of her role in it were circumscribed by the church's teachings with all their social and cultural implications for women and her own experience. Considering the lack of opportunity for women to be educated, we can hardly wonder at the Wife of Bath's boisterous and cantankerous declaration " 'Experience, though noon auctoritee / Were in this world, is right ynogh for me."[23] Unlike the saints whom Petroff describes as living in loving, supportive communities, sharing their remarkable experiences daily, Margery suffers from a sense of isolation and ignorance, as indicated throughout her *Book*. She is always conscious of the solitary role she has chosen as a laywoman and aware of her limitations as a teacher, determined by her gender and illiteracy. How could her knowledge of the world, and of her own spirituality, be other than experiential?

Franciscan meditation, as we have seen in the gospel harmonies, was considered a valid way of knowing about Christ that for the simple penitent was more important than the intellectual comprehension of dogmatic truths. Margery's meditations stem from a deeply Franciscan tradition of divinely inspired knowledge; in chapter 11 of the *Legenda*

---

[22] Petroff, *Consolation of the Blessed*, p. 81.
[23] Geoffrey Chaucer, *The Wife of Bath's Tale*, lines 1–2, in *The Works of Geoffrey Chaucer*, 2d ed., ed. F. N. Robinson, p. 76.

maior, Bonaventure explains the mystery of a natural knowledge of God. Although Francis "had no skill in Sacred Scripture acquired through study," he was blessed with a knowledge which he derived from his loving meditations on Christ's Passion, for "where the scholarship of the teacher stands outside, the affection of the lover entered within."[24]

Francis makes clear, however, that all knowledge is important only if it helps men and women "to practice what they have heard and when they have put it into practice themselves to propose it to others likewise."[25] Meditations on the Gospels and knowledge of scripture, therefore, should first urge *imitatio*, rather than a hunger for more knowledge. The end of all affective devotion is to arouse a reciprocal love in the penitent, who recognizes the great love in the sacrifice made for humankind.

Francis's own conversion was not complete until one day, while praying in a secluded spot, he suddenly had a miraculous vision of Christ crucified.[26] Francis interpreted this apparition as a divine injunction to imitate Christ in the world. He thus came to a personal understanding of perfect charity through experience, and the rest of his life he devoted himself and his order to the Passion.

Margery's awakening from madness to a vision of Christ sitting beside her on her bed is similar. At this time Christ appears not crucified but clad in a purple-silk mantle; nonetheless, he reproves Margery's lack of faith with words echoing his own on the cross, thus reminding her of his constant love and hence her obligation to him: "Dowtyr, why hast þow forsakyn me, and I forsoke neuyr þe?" (p. 8, line 21).

This consoling vision brings Margery back to health, and she decides that she will be Christ's "seruawnt" (p. 9, line 9). What she does not admit readily, however, is the utter sacrifice required of those who serve

[24] Bonaventure, *Legenda S. Francisci*, chap. 11, par. 1, p. 535. The Latin reads: "Penetrabat enim ab omni labe purum ingenium mysteriorum abscondita, et ubi magistralis scienta foris stat, affectus introibat amantis."

[25] Ibid. The Latin reads: "Mihi quidem placet, dum tamen exemplo Christi, qui magis orasse legitur quam legisse, orationis studium non omittant nec tantum studeant, ut sciant, qualiter debeant loqui, sed ut audita faciant, et cum fecerint, aliis facienda proponant."

[26] Ibid., chap. 1, par. 5, p. 507.

Christ. Consequently she continues to indulge her pride and vanity. Since her husband cannot satisfy her taste for luxury and social prominence, Margery seeks worldly comfort through her "huswyfre" as an independent businesswoman (p. 10, line 11). She is thus uncertain of the meaning of "service," until one Friday before Christmas, as she kneels, miserable and despondent, in a chapel in Saint Margaret's, in Lynne, she has a sudden illumination of the significance of Christ's Passion. This episode marks Margery's true conversion and acceptance of her vocation to imitate Christ in the world. She is not called, as might be expected of a religious woman in her time and place, to live the contemplative or enclosed life; rather, she is commanded to leave her beads and to wear a hairshirt in her "hert" (p. 17, line 8). Margery is told that, like Christ, she will be tormented and challenged by the "pepul of þe world" (p. 17, line 16). Clearly Margery accepts the vocation of a lay Tertiary, even if she is not specifically so called. From this time Margery relies on her meditative visions of Christ's life and Passion as a source of comfort and affirmation of her choice: "After her full conversion she never shrinks from the practical acts of service, but it is always service growing from colloquy, which in turn grows out of the most vivid meditative awareness of Christ."[27]

Margery's detailed accounts of her Christocentric meditations allow us to peer into the most private depths of her spirituality; here alone can we come to comprehend how the sorrowful image of the cross brought Margery to a full understanding of her relationship with Christ. They also provide a penetrating view of late medieval "affectivism," and how the simple but evocative lyrics and descriptions of the Passion in sermons drew laypersons to confession. On her first pilgrimage to Jerusalem, Margery has a special illumination on Mount Calvary after she envisions Christ "Hangyn befor hir bodily eye in hys manhode" (p. 70, lines 6–7). The image recalls the pitiful spectacle so common in fourteenth- and fifteenth-century paintings (p. 70, lines 10–17):

> ...hys precyows tendyr body, alto-rent & toryn wyth scorgys, mor ful of wowndys þan euyr was duffehows of holys... þe gresly & grevous wownde in hys precyows syde schedyng owt blood & watyr for hir lofe & hir salvacyon.

[27] Thornton, *Margery Kempe*, p. 43.

Through this vision Margery receives the gift of "pyte & compassyon" that is the source of her conviction throughout the rest of her *Book* (p. 70, line 22). Like all other Christocentric devotion, Margery's meditation focuses on the disparity between human and divine love by placing Christ's death in the context of human loss and grief through the death of a friend. Following upon her compunction and remorse for Christ's suffering, Margery contemplates her own weeping and indirectly gives an eloquent exposition on the proper response of all believers to Christ crucified (p. 70, lines 28–35):

> . . .ʒyf her frendys er partyn fro hem, þei wyl cryen & roryn and wryngen her handys as ʒyf þei had no wytte ne non mende . . . &, ʒyf a man cownsel hem to leevyn er seesyn of her wepyng er crying, þei wyl seyn þat þei may not; þei louyd her frend so meche & he was so gentyl & so kende to hem þat þei may be no wey for-ʒetyn hym.

It is her inability to forget Christ in her daily life that best charac-terizes Margery Kempe's spirituality. When, in a church in Norwich, Margery beholds a "fayr ymage of owr Lady clepyd a pyte," she immedi-ately begins to meditate on the Passion and is found by a baffled priest, weeping "as þei sche xulde a deyd" (p. 148; lines 5–10). Either to console or to rebuke her, the priest claims: "Damsel, Ihesu is ded long sithyn" (p. 148, lines 10–11). Margery's famous reproving reply illus-trates the way all external symbols or images came to point to the greater reality of the cross in her life: "Sir, hys deth is as fresch to me as he had deyd þis same day, & so me thynketh it awt to be to ʒow & to alle Cristen pepil" (p. 148, lines 13–15).

In her *Book*, Margery Kempe describes her spiritual maturation in terms of vision and exemplarism, celebrating her growing sensitivity to God's presence in everyday life in a manner reminiscent of Bonaven-ture's account of Francis' development (p. 172, lines 11–15):

> So be processe of tyme hir mende & hir thowt was so ioynyd to God þat sche neuyr forʒate hym but contynualy had mende of hym & behelde hym in alle creaturys. & euyr þe mor þat sche encrysd in lofe and in deuocyon, þe mor sche encresyd in sorwe & in contrycyon.

At this point in her life the tangible realities — a mother and child, a leper, or a priest bearing the "precyows Sacrament . . . a-bowte þe town" — all point to Christ's Passion and elicit a compassionate response from Margery (p. 172, line 30). Like Francis, she seems equally to inhabit a spiritual world and the flesh-and-blood world whose language translates the miraculous and transcendent for fallen humanity. She also shares Francis's deep love for all creatures, the breadth of her charity extending to all of creation (p. 69, lines 1–8):

> & su*m*tyme, whan sche saw þe Crucyfyx, er yf sche sey a man had a wownde er a best
> wheþyr it wer, er ȝyf a man bett a childe be-for hir er smet an hors er an-oþer best
> wyth a whippe, ȝyf sche myth sen it er heryn it, hir thowt sche saw owyr Lord be
> betyn er wowndyd lyk as sche saw in þe man er in þe best, as wel in þe feld as in þe
> town, & be hir-selfe (a)lone as wel as a-mong þe pepyl.

Margery's interpretation of pain and suffering and her recollective compassion thus accord with Francis's own vividly incarnational spirituality: "He often paid to ransom lambs that were being led to their death, remembering that most gentle lamb who willed to be led to slaughter to pay the ransom of sinners."[28]

The attraction their dramatic piety held for laypersons was its transforming power: seeing Christ in all of creation and its attendant mysteries encouraged the penitent to profess an active love. Margery explains this with eloquent simplicity to the belligerent mayor of Leicester, who accused her of hypocrisy (p. 115, lines 32–33):

> For I do ȝow to wetyn, ser, þat þer is no man in þis worlde þat I lofe so meche as
> God, for I lofe hym a-bouyn al thynge, &, ser, I telle ȝow trewly I lofe al men in God
> & for God.

Margery's spiritual experiences granted her a redeemed perspective that conflicted with the mayor's limited, earthbound view of circumstances. She shared this ability to discern the spiritual realities that give meaning to the physical world with other medieval visionaries, most of whom were saints or had religious callings, like Julian of Norwich. But such illumination was not limited to those in religious orders. In her study of medieval perception Carolly Erikson stresses that intellectual understanding and learning are not necessarily the criteria for a meaningful vision or meditation:

---

[28] Bonaventure, *Legenda S. Francisci*, chap. 8, par. 6, p. 527. The Latin reads: "Redemit frequenter agnos, qui ducebantur ad mortem, illius memor Agni mitissimi, qui ad occisionem duci voluit pro peccatoribus redimendis."

> Absolute sight, the vision of the substance or essence of things was withheld from most men, but not participation in the visionary climate of medieval culture. Imaginative visual habits broadened their range of perception. Informative visions gave them guidance and nourished their faith; illuminative visions clarified and deepened their understanding.[29]

Margery's meditations on Christ's life and death certainly functioned in the latter ways. Because her visions led her to an extreme desire to imitate Christ literally, however, Roland Maisonneuve believes that, with Saint Francis, Margery belongs in a special and long-neglected category of mystics known as "fools of God."[30] He characterizes these childlike souls as holy people who participate in Christ's life through symbolic and external gestures.[31] They share a simple faith and are thus propelled on a "never-ending pilgrimage," teaching compassion and penance through their dual lives of prayer and works.[32] In the *Book*, for example, Margery has a vision of Christ in which he assures her (p. 183, lines 18–21):

> þat any creatur in erthe, haf he be neuyr so horrybyl a synner, he thar neuyr fallyn in despeyr ȝyf he wyl takyn exampil of thy leuyng & werkyn sumwhat þeraftyr as he may do.

Although Margery is unique, the imagistic nature of her spiritual experiences points to a general connection between the "democratization of mysticism" in the late Middle Ages, of which Heiko Obermann speaks, and the Franciscan evangelical movement that proposed vision as a means for all Christians to experience, and thus know, God.[33] Whether or not Margery was truly a mystic, she has long held a place with the English mystics because of her colloquies and visions and their

[29] Erikson, *The Medieval Vision*, p. 46.
[30] Maissoneve, "Margery Kempe and the Eastern and Western Tradition," p. 1.
[31] Ibid., p. 5.
[32] Ibid., p. 4.
[33] Heiko A. Obermann, "The Shape of Late Medieval Thought: The Birthpangs of the Modern Era," in Heiko A. Obermann and Charles Trinkhaus, eds., *The Pursuit of Holiness in Late Medieval and Renaissance Religion*, p. 19. Also, for a discussion of Margery's place in the tradition of Continental female piety see Susan Dickman, "Margery Kempe and the Continental Tradition of the Pious Woman," in Marion Glasscoe, ed., *The Medieval Mystical Tradition in England*, Papers Read at Dartington Hall, July, 1984, pp. 150–168.

effect on her life.[34] We may even have to reassess our definitions of the *via positiva*, or the predominately Western, incarnational mysticism of Julian or Richard Rolle in this light. Modern scholars seem to revere the *via negativa*—the nonvisual, utterly passive and unitive experience of God, best exemplified in *The Cloud of Unknowing*, as the highest form of mysticism.[35] Louis Dupré, however, in *A Search for the Meaning of Religious Attitudes*, questions this exclusive definition of mysticism with its emphasis on the rare and isolated experience of God:

> There are other advantages in considering mysticism an aspect of salvation. Not the least of them is that it returns the mystical experience to the mainstream of religious life. The term "mystical" is not usually restricted to exceptional and strictly private states of ecstacy. But it permeates the entire religious experience.[36]

Dupré points out that this hunger for communion with the transcendent is the key element in all religions—a fact that the Franciscans recognized. Furthermore, the term "mystical" was not always as narrowly applied to religious men and women as we presently conceive it to be. The flood of female mystics in thirteenth-century Germany, as described by Jacques de Vitry in his commentary on convent life, seems abnormally high to us only because we have come to view mysticism as a private, rather than communal, experience.[37] Julian of Norwich, for

[34] See Richard Kieckhefer, *Unquiet Souls*, p. 94. While Kieckhefer's discussion on devotion to the Passion concerns fourteenth-century hagiography, it is particularly applicable to Margery Kempe's own devotional methods, for she clearly was influenced by the women saints' lives of her own day. Kiekhoffer lucidly addresses the question of the "truth" of imagined scenes or dramatic meditations: "It would clearly be futile to seek out any factual basis for these incidents, but at times one suspects that the vision narrative was a hagiographic device for describing less exceptional meditative experience. . . . [it] is less clear whether meditation was the occasion for what the biographer is claiming as a genuine vision or whether the vision-narrative is (as one might suspect) a way of talking about the meditation." I agree with Kieckhefer's conclusion that "neither the saint nor the hagiographer would have felt compelled to distinguish rigidly between humanly induced meditation and divinely bestowed vision, especially since even the former would be seen as ultimately aroused by grace."

[35] Maissoneuve, "Margery Kempe and the Eastern and Western Tradition," p. 1.

[36] Louis Dupré, *The Other Dimension: A Search for the Meaning of Religious Attitudes*, p. 484. See chap. 12, "The Mystical Vision," pp. 484–545.

[37] For an introductory discussion of visionary activity in women's communities on the continent see Brenda M. Bolton, "Mulieres sanctae," in *Sanctity and Secularity: The Church and the World*, Studies in Church History, vol. 10, pp. 77–95.

example, fulfills our expectations of the mystic in her hermetic solitude, her private persona, and her reticence about revealing her visions to others.

We have yet to decide how to read Margery's accounts of her meditative and contemplative visions, taking into account her popular and experiential education and lay status. One cannot but notice that Christian tradition associates mysticism with the pure contemplative life and, therefore, cenobitic monasticism. Since such a life was regarded as essentially male and was considered difficult for women because it required one to be both educable (hence rational) and chaste, women are generally not included in this tradition. [38] We regard Hildegard von Bingen and Julian of Norwich, women clearly educated in intellectual and hence monastic traditions, as valid mystics because they belong to this world of confined, virginal, and intellectual religious experience. A bourgeois laywoman like Margery cannot meet such traditional requirements of mystics.

With Francis's emergence on the Western religious scene and his "experiential" approach to private spirituality, deeply instilled in the mendicant life and passed on to the lay Tertiaries, we have a new development in mysticism — or, as Obermann notes, its "democratization." The Franciscans taught the uneducated laity personal and experiential devotional exercises, providing a new consciousness of private spiritual development. Works like the *Meditations on the Life of Christ* consciously created parallels between the life of all believers and Christ's historical life achieved through visual meditation. While Margery does not specifically refer to the *Meditations*, her editors hypothesize that she was familiar with the work, most likely in Nicholas Love's translation. [39]

[38] Vern L. Bullough, "Medieval Medical and Scientific Views of Women," *Viator* 4 (1973): 497. Bullough points out that although the Church recognized the need for multiplying the human race and woman's functional role in procreation, it considered virginity as *man's* highest nature. Sexuality was viewed not only as morally dangerous but also as irrational desire. Monasticism, therefore, eventually came to identify rationality with celibacy. For women, as a result, virginity became the "easiest way to approach the male level of rationality."

[39] In reference to Margery's dramatic meditations on the Passion, Hope Emily Allen writes that "there can be no doubt that Margery knew the great work so long ascribed to St. Bonaventura" and assumes that Nicholas Love's translation was probably read to her. See Kempe, *The Book of Margery Kempe*, p. 333. Also see Atkinson, *Mystic and Pilgrim*, pp. 151–155.

Margery's vivid meditative experiences, "altogether of her time," confirmed her perilous path of *imitatio* in the face of authority and were consequently the spiritual nuclei of her existence.[40] However extraordinary she may seem to us, in many respects she was an average uneducated laywoman who reaped the benefits from affective devotional exercises intended as a prepenitential device. Many of her meditations on gospel events follow "classical models" created specifically for uneducated women by Anselm.[41] Such meditations, popularized by the Bonaventuran tradition, allowed Margery to come to a sense of herself, of her own spiritual nature, and compelled her to act in her own world in order to change people's lives for the better. In this sense she was very much like the female saints of whom Petroff speaks, those who, by breaking social rules and displaying an exceptional independence, assumed the responsibility for their own and others' spiritual welfare.

For women like Margery and Ghirardesca, visions of Christ's life, and the Crucifixion especially, redefined passivity, transforming into a religious ideal the role their respective cultures assigned to them; from the self-annihilation that comes from meditation on the Passion and identification with the suffering Virgin springs a new sense of self that demands to be tested through acts, or imitation of Christ's life in the world.[42]

In the thirteenth century the church denied women the privilege of literally following Francis's footsteps; Francis himself was utterly conventional in wishing to enclose the sister order, the Poor Clares, and devised a rule for them that would regularize their existence. We can see from Petroff's accounts of the Italian female saints that they would not be constrained. They assume male costume; Ghirardesca puts on a cowl and accompanies a monk on a visit to another monastery.[43] They find themselves spirited in dreams and often physically out of their enclosed residences. The determined search for an intimate knowledge of God, which Francis guarded in his own Rule by his refusal to

[40] Colledge, *The Medieval Mystics in England*, p. 219.
[41] Ibid.
[42] Petroff, *Consolation of the Blessed*, p. 66.
[43] Ibid., p. 114.

legislate a specific kind of prayer life, was sought as eagerly by women of the thirteenth century who had to rely only on visual meditation.

In the beginning of her *Book*, Margery sketches a disturbingly distorted self-portrait: plagued by fears of damnation and a shameful sense of her inadequacy, she unsuccessfully attempts to appease her anxieties by "fastyng bred & watyr & oþer dedys of almes wyth devowt preyers" (p. 7, lines 6–7). It is Margery's lack of faith in the cleansing power of confession, her fear that her sin is too great a burden even for the cross to bear, that leads her to the despair and madness that signify both spiritual and physical sickness.

We do not know the specific nature of Margery's great sin, but sensitive scholars like Clarissa Atkinson assume that it was sexual.[44] If so, Margery's sense of isolation and rejection from the body of healthy, shriven believers results from her natural role as a sexual being in the highly problematic position that women shared in the medieval church. It is hardly an exaggeration to say that it was almost as difficult for a woman to pass into heaven during the Middle Ages as it was for a camel to pass through the eye of a needle in Christ's day. Margery's introduction sets the *topos* of her tale of conversion (p. 1, lines 26–28; page 2, lines 1–4):

> Thus alle þis thyngys turnyng up-so-down, þis creatur whych many ȝerys had gon wyl & euyr ben vnstable was parfythly drawen & steryd to entren þe wey of hy perfeccyon, whech parfyth wey Cryst ower Savyowr in hys propyr persoone examplyd. Sadly he trad it & dewly he went it beforn.

Margery's conversion is depicted in terms of action — or *imitatio*. She seeks truth disclosed through private revelation and an internalized knowledge derived from her own experience, not from the authoritative voices that offered her a very conditional, rather than unconditional, intimacy with Christ. The *Book* is Margery's exhaustive effort to validate her highly individual religious illumination, the success of which seemed unlikely because of the choices she had already made, or had been compelled to make, such as marrying and giving birth to fourteen children.

Margery voices her anxieties about her loss of virginity and thus her

---

[44] Atkinson, *Mystic and Pilgrim*, p. 212.

loss of spiritual privileges early in her autobiography before she finds her own spiritual expression and identity. Facing another pregnancy, she rightfully concedes in one of her many meditative dialogues with Christ that she has surrendered any chance of attaining the ideal, or unviolated spiritual state of virginity by which women emulate "male" rationality in the face of sexual or irrational desire[45]: "Lord Ihesu, þis maner of leuyng longyth to thy holy maydens" (p. 48, line 35). Christ's response is comforting. While the various states of human existence are hierarchical and qualified, Christ's love is unqualified. Maidenhood is "mor parfyt & mor holy þan þe state of wedewhode" and "þe state of wedewhode more parfyt þan þe state [of] wedlake" (p. 49, lines 5–7). Good, like Christ's love, is boundless and immeasurable: "Ʒet dowtyr I lofe ʒe as wel as any mayden in þe world. Þer may no man let me to lofe whom I wyl & as mech as I wyl" (p. 49, lines 7–8). Perhaps most comforting of all, Christ takes heed of potential: "I take non hede what a man hath ben, but I take hede what he wyl ben" (p. 49, lines 20–21).

For Margery this transformation of the will from a wayward, erring defiance of God to a positive force that grants her power to effect change in God's favor means assurance of spiritual health in spite of the dogmatic limits placed on woman's spiritual capabilities and human interpretations of her role. Her spiritual independence in seeking the difficult balance between the active and the contemplative lives, however, baffled her contemporaries and caused many to question her orthodoxy. Lollard women were also characterized by an openly evangelical approach to their vocations. As a result Margery's orthodoxy was most heatedly debated by her countrymen in England and abroad.[46] Both men and women remarked with hostility on the impropriety of Margery's wandering, as well as the presumptuousness of her teaching. A frustrated intolerance often characterized the attitudes of her tormentors. Unable to "define" Margery's behavior by placing her in those

[45] Bullough, "Medieval Medical and Scientific Views of Women," p. 497.

[46] On Lollard women's activity in Margery's day see Claire Cross, "Great Reasoners in Scripture: The Activities of Women Lollards 1380–1530," in Derek Baker, ed., *Medieval Women*, p. 378. Also see Maureen Fries, "Margery Kempe," in Paul Szarmach, ed., *An Introduction to the Medieval Mystics of Europe*, p. 220. Fries notes: "The Lollard feminism of Margery's day, approving even of female priests (at least in theory), was eminently suited to Magery's own idea of her vocation."

roles appropriate for either religious women or laywomen, her contemporaries felt threatened by her.[47]

A monk at Canterbury to whom Margery rehearsed "a story of Scriptur" vehemently rebuked her audacity, claiming "I wold þow wer closyd in an hows of ston þat þer schuld no man speke wyth þe" (p. 27, lines 31–33). The proper place for a woman of religion was the anchoress's cell, which represented death to the world. Similarly troubled by Margery's holy "dalliance" with Christ, the steward of Leicester, who held Margery for questioning, pronounced a verdict "as many mon had do be-forn": "Eyþyr þu art a ryth good woman er ellys a ryth wikked woman" (p. 113, lines 30–31). Nonetheless, his indecision served as protection to Margery when she was subject to his obscene gestures and insinuations, until he released her to the kindly jailer and his wife.

Nor can women be absolved from the suspicion and cruelty with which Margery was often received; the *Book* is indeed a revealing testament of the bitterly fearful religious climate, illuminating the strain of conservatism that characterized much fifteenth-century religious literature. Arrested by two yeoman of the duke of Bedford, Margery is taken to Beverly to submit to questioning about her religious practices. As she walks through the streets, "women cam rennyng out of her howsys wyth her rokkys, crying to þe pepil, 'Brenneyth þis fals heretyk'" (p. 129, lines 30–31).

Margery was examined in her "articles of faith" both in Leicester and in York and proved that her religious views were entirely othodox. It was the way she chose to profess her beliefs, rather than the beliefs themselves, that caused the consternation described throughout her *Book*. Ultimately, without intentionally diminishing loyalty to the church, her *Book* insists on the superior claim of God upon the individual soul to that of any human institution.

Margery's sense of oppression, derived from the monastic perspective of women that defined her role in society, could not be confined to the world about her, which demanded her silence. Her need to justify herself was much more deeply-rooted. Even in her meditations she asserted her primary loyalties, clarifying her spiritual values and vocation (p. 175, lines 5–9):

[47] Atkinson, *Mystic and Pilgrim*, p. 50.

Anoþer tyme þe seyd creatur beheld how owr Lady was, hir thowt, in deying & all þe apostleys knelyng be-forn hir & askyng grace. Þan she cryid & wept sor. Þe apostelys comawndyd hir to cesyn & be stille.

Margery's refusal to be silenced by the apostles she reveres suggests that she fears rejection and suppression even in the imaginative realm of visual meditation. In spite of her commitment to the church, she feels threatened by the male hierarchy on all levels. She will allow nothing to interfere with her relationship with Christ and the Virgin, and the sense of personal guidance she derives from such relationships takes precedence over all others.

Whatever Margery's veiled agonies or thinly disguised insecurities, her visual meditations and the manner in which she weaves them into her book become ways of recognizing and dealing with spiritual torpor; the *Book* thus becomes "an instrument of healing."[48] Her meditations parallel the external voyages Margery undertakes in her life. Both her meditations and her pilgrimages are recounted carthartically, and are consciously revised or "re-created."[49]

Because Margery's narrative synthesizes all experience, the order or design she adopts to tell her life gives as much meaning to her work as her professions of faith. The sources for her narrative structure range from popular gospel harmonies to the continental female saints' lives and are difficult to pinpoint with exactitude. Nevertheless, the spiritual movement of Margery's life is a journey from "a position of subjection to tradition toward one of incipient control."[50] She transforms her spiritual role from that of a laywoman without an honored vocation to one especially beloved by Christ. Paradoxically, Margery finds freedom and a means of expressing her spirituality through service and the subjection of her will to God's; that is the essence of the Franciscan way of life and the progressive movement of her *Book*.

By the end of the text Margery has affirmed her ability to make her life whole by yoking her history to the Christian conversional pattern

[48] Hope Phyllis Weissman, "Margery Kempe in Jerusalem: *Hysterica Compassio* in the Late Middle Ages," in Mary J. Carruthers and Elizabeth D. Kirk, eds., *Acts of Interpretation: The Text in Its Contexts, 700–1600: Essays in Honor of E. Talbot Donaldson*, p. 201.

[49] Ibid.

[50] Ibid.

that the gospel harmonies portrayed as the path to inward and outward imitation of Christ. From her conversion during Advent, the season of spiritual harmony and rebirth, Margery shows her spiritual childhood transforming into a mature faith as she moves toward a full understanding of the Passion. In illustrating this process, the *Book* "aligns her activities with established scriptural and extrascriptural materials."[51] While the chronological order in Margery's narrative is confusing, her narrative always acknowledges "spiritual" time in the form of the liturgical year and the events of Christ's life on which the liturgy is based. These are the patterns that come to give meaning to and provide a context for Margery's spiritual growth. In "aligning" her own history with this cycle, Margery does not discover her individuality in a modern sense but comes to accept the preordained path to conversion and salvation, accepting what she perceives as God's will manifested in history. For Margery, peace and stability result from harmonizing the inner and outer self, or the active and contemplative lives. Her meditations confirm that the Christian path is one of interior and exterior *peregrinatio*, a long and tiring journey to Jerusalem.

While Margery often used the terms "contemplacyon" and "medytacyon" interchangeably when describing her visions of gospel events, she clearly practiced only meditation—the lowest form of mental prayer, whose fruits are primarily moral.[52] Like Ghirardesca, Margery learned that imaginative meditation and the extemporaneous creation of sacred scenes led her to the threshold of a more immediate spiritual realm than had hitherto been permitted to women, or to laypersons. Her visions substantiated her often perilous task of conformity to Christ. Ultimately, like those of the Poor Clares for whom the *Meditations* was written, Margery's visual meditations initiated her into a body of the spiritual elect previously circumscribed by the liturgically rich life of the monastery or the mendicant life prohibited to women. Margery's prayer life was clearly ordered by the liturgical year of the church, which gave a psychic rhythm to the daily lives of the enclosed religious. We recollect the author of the *Meditations* carefully structuring the meditative experience of his spiritual daughter to synchronize the liturgical

---

[51] Ibid., p. 205.
[52] *The Catholic Encyclopedia*, 12:348.

season of the year with the sacramental order of the week, and the events in Christ's historical life on which both are based. Similarly, in the years Margery covers in her *Book*, we are always conscious of the ebb and flow of the liturgical seasons in their cyclic continuum, marking not the process of aging and decay but Margery's spiritual coming of age. Margery remembers events by the observed religious seasons and feasts that dramatically divide the year for medieval people: Lent, Easter, Lammas Tide, and the Feast of Corpus Christi.

Margery's meditations naturally take their subject matter from the seasons and the corresponding scriptural themes that were so ingrained in her mind after years of sacramental worship. That is not unusual in itself; the Poor Clares did as much. What is unusual is the way Margery's meditations outwardly confirm her conversion, with its accompanying hardships and humiliations, and finally her firm identification with Christ's humility and Passion. Her internal spiritual development manifests itself in a biographical pattern similar to that of the gospel harmonies. Thus the Nativity scene in Margery's autobiography occurs appropriately after her conversion. Similarly, her lengthy depiction of the Passion toward the end of the *Book* also conforms schematically to the harmonies, which, in keeping with the Franciscan "idea that the Passion is in itself the font of effectual grace," devoted the largest portion of their texts to this episode.[53] Whether consciously or unconsciously, Margery narrates her experiences in a manner reminiscent of the *Meditations*, ordering the pivotal events in her life to parallel the Scriptures and treating other events as parables of her ministry, their moral truths existing above and outside a temporal framework.

In the nativity episode, which occurs soon after she recovers from despair, Margery seeks divine guidance in finding the best subject for her meditation. Christ directs her to think of the young Virgin Mary in the Gospels, her faith newly tried, in preparation for his birth. Margery's vision is not the reverent, stylized portrayal of the Nativity that Bonaventure sketches in his own meditative *Lignum vitae*. Rather, Margery imagines a hurried sequence of events that begins with her trip to Jerusalem and culminates in her daily begging for food and procure-

[53] Jeffrey, *The Early English Lyric and Franciscan Spirituality*, p. 54.

ment of "herborwe" for the Virgin (p. 19, line 11). These concerns reflect Margery's sense of economy, her merchant upbringing, and her often businesslike approach to securing her daily bread. To unsympathetic readers of her *Book*, Margery's personal interpretation of these sacred events, in which she assumes an imaginative role, may well have seemed like presumptuous toying with the biblical text.

As the *Meditations* advises, however, Margery dramatically transforms the gospel narrative into a profoundly moving spiritual experience. We may question the ontological nature of Margery's "gostly syghtys," her literalism, her dramatic, often overtly feminine translation of salvation history, but cannot doubt that her meditations achieved their purpose in inciting her to penance and imitation (p. 192, lines 26–31):

> And þan hir thowt þe Iewys spokyn a-geyn boystowsly to owr Lady & put hir a-way fro hir Sone. Þan þe forseyd creatur thowt þat sche cryid owt of þe Iewys & seyd, "Ʒe cursyd Iewys, why sle ye my Lord Ihesu Crist? Sle me raþar & late hym gon."

In her profusely emotional response, Margery asks a probing question that speaks particularly to the laypeople of her age, who are awakening to a hunger for order and stability which, as Langland professed earlier, begins in a spiritual awareness of self and Christian obligation: "What xal we now don & how xal we beryn þis gret sorwe þat we xal have for thy lofe?" (p. 193, lines 9–10).

Ultimately, for Margery the path of righteousness is one of *imitatio*, and shortly thereafter she answers her question herself. The *Meditations* advises penitents to comfort the Virgin after the Crucifixion; in her homely meditation Margery guides the Virgin home and makes "for owr Lady a good cawdel & browt it hir to comfortyn hir" (p. 195, lines 7–8). In her own life Margery, vermin-ridden and suffering the "many scornys of wyfys of Rome" after her return from a pilgrimage to Assisi, begs for food for an impoverished widow and "seruyd hir as sche wolde a don owyr Lady" (p. 85, lines 31–37).

The apex of Margery Kempe's spiritual experience is marked by the gift of tears she receives when, physically on "þe mount of Calvarye," she envisions the Crucifixion "wyth hir bodyly ey" (p. 68, lines 9–12). We may feel some distaste at Margery's physical reaction to this meditative scene; her body is wracked and tormented in utter sympathy with

Christ's pain as revealed in her vision. Nonetheless, the vision, en-
hanced by the sacredness of the place, provides a spiritual and historical
referent from which Margery gains penitential fervor throughout the
remainder of her life (p. 184, lines 26–32):

> Many ȝerys on Palme Sonday, as þis creatur was at þe processyon wyth oþer good
> pepyl in þe chirch-ȝerd & beheld how þe preystys dedyn her obseruawnce, how þei
> knelyd to þe Sacrament & þe pepil also, it semyd to hir gostly syght as þei sche had
> ben þat tyme in Ierusalem & seen owr Lord in hys manhod receyuyd of þe pepil as he
> was whil he went her in erth.

We must look further, however, to discern how this ability to internalize the events related in the Gospels through meditation, and to
fictionalize Scripture, ultimately leads to another creative act—that of
re-creating a life, or an autobiography. The Franciscan process of
embellishing, or imagining, the Gospels to arouse feelings necessary
for compunction of heart, of fictively participating in scriptural scenes,
is reflexive; it reverts to the self and the individual's desire to recast the
life of the converted sinner into a pattern more acceptable to God.
Soon after her conversion, for example, Margery "ymagyned" or envisioned her own martyrdom (p. 30, line 3).[54] Clearly there is no factual
truth in this grisly scene of Margery's beheading; instead, the vision
becomes the occasion for a meditative colloquy with Christ whereby
Margery examines her own steadfastness. In the same way Margery
revises scriptural scenes, gazing upon herself as she participates or
responds to them. This self-absorption has been reduced erroneously
to "vanity."[55] Margery's meditations and spiritual autobiography share
a penitential theme; their purpose lies in "re-visioning" or re-creating
all of Margery's thoughts and experiences from an enlightened
perspective.

Margery's *Book* chronicles an utter transformation from a wealthy
woman of Lynn, anxiously seeking security in worldly possessions and

---

[54] *MED*, s.v. *Imaginen*, a.: "To form a mental picture of something not present." In
Margery's case, this fiction is clearly a meditation in which she explores her ability to
surrender her will entirely to God's, even in the extreme case of martyrdom. Although
in all probability the image was inspired by scenes from popular hagiography, the
question of its fictionality and Margery's role as the creator of narrative becomes central
in our understanding of the *Book* itself and its function.

[55] Kempe, *The Book of Margery Kempe*, p. lxiv.

status, like Paul or Francis, to one who serves the poor with "neyther peny ne half-peny" in the belief that she will be provided for (p. 92, line 29). Through the comfort and guidance Christ provides in her meditations, Margery assumes the role of one dispossessed, wholly acknowledging the necessity to "folwyn þe steppys of owr Lord Ihesu Crist" literally (p. 107, lines 31–32). The end of the *Book* is largely an account emphasizing this change and sets up a complete contrast from the character we first know in the *Book*. We can see a connection between Margery's actions and her meditations in this section, which reveals the spiritual source of the stability that comes to represent conversion to Margery. Rather than a "reedspyr whech boweth wyt*h* eue*ry* wynd & neu*yr* is stable," Margery is strong enough to minister cheerfully to those in need, regardless of her own desires and fears (p. 1, lines 20–21).

When Christ tells Margery that he will "pr*e*yn myn owyn Modir to beggyn for þe," for example, Margery willingly adopts a life of poverty, begging "hir mete fro dor to dore" (p. 93, line 1; p. 94, line 6). Exposed to the abject poverty of Rome, Margery proves her sincerity in wishing to live according to the apostolic injunction; she does not recoil from hunger and disease but thanks God "hyly of þe pouerte þat sche was in, trusting þerthowr to be p*ar*tynyr wyth hem in m*e*ryte" (p. 94, lines 23–25). In her zeal to be obedient Margery gives away not only all her own goods but also those of her disgruntled companion, Richard the broken-backed.

The harmony of her inner and outer life, her merciful acts and their source in her imaginative visions of the Gospels, is perhaps best illustrated in Margery's role as mourner of the dead for the community that ultimately spurns her (p. 172, lines 35–37; p. 173, lines 1–2):

> Also þe sayd creatur was desiryd of mech pepil to be wyt*h* hem at her deying & to pr*e*y for hem, for, þow þei louyd not hir wepyng ne hir crying in her lyfe-tyme, þei de[si]ryd þ*at* sche xulde bothyn wepyn & cryin whan þei xulde deyin, & so sche dede.

The ingratitude of the people who caused her physical and emotional anguish in her search for a holier life does not prove to be a heavy burden for Margery. As if to confirm that this act of generosity is simply her Christian responsibility, the scene that follows in her text is a meditation in which "hir thowt sche saw owr Lord deyin & sum-tyme owr Lady.... Þan xulde sche cryin, wepyn, & sobbyn ful wondirfully as sche had be-heldyn owr Lord in hys deying er our Lady in hir deying" (p. 173, lines 5–9).

If Margery's meditation is characteristic of devotional practices, we can assume that those who generally practiced visual, participatory meditation created "fictional" biographical experiences, or biblical scenes that were really self-conscious narratives that explored individual spirituality and responses to Christ. Affective devotion functions as a mirror; the penitent, encountering Christ crucified, examines his or her own wayward desires and actions. From this penitential process comes a more intimate relationship with Christ.

Margery's *Book* is perhaps unique in that it challenges the Augustinian conception of spiritual development as a linear process. Her book does not conform to that pattern of conversion, or to the hierarchically schematized movement that conceptually structures Bonaventure's *Itinerarium* and Francis's *Legenda maior*. Margery's *Book* reflects a different kind of struggle — one acknowledging that few are granted beatific visions and yet that all can participate in a transcendent reality. For most, the road to a personal knowledge of God meanders, wanders, and grows faint at times, in the organic, experiential movement exhibited by Margery's memory. While Margery initially adopts the "conversion" pattern of hagiography — Paul's and Augustine's — her experiences reveal that the path to salvation is cyclical, like the liturgical year, an idea expressed most movingly in *Pearl*. The human compulsion toward sin negates the possibility of unhampered movement to perfection. That is why penance is as crucial after "conversion" as before. Francis's biographers vehemently admit the constant temptations against which he struggled after his dramatic conversion. Nor are these battles always depicted as external dramas, as in early Christian hagiography such as the Old English *Juliana*, where the devil assumes the guise of a pagan prince, or his earthly form. Francis conquers pride and a lust for sexual and other physical comforts. In the *Fioretti*, for example, Francis's sanctity never diminishes the reality of "Brother Ass" — the physical limitations of the human condition.

Margery's dark vision of men exposing their "membrys un-to hir" occurs late in her *Book*, and is a chastisement for being willful (p. 145, line 14). Because Margery refuses to believe that God wishes to show her the fates of other men and women, damnation or salvation, she is nearly driven to despair with "þes horrybyl syghtys," which Clarissa Atkinson reminds us are the inversion of male visions of sexual temptation in many saints' lives (p. 145, line 22).[56] At this time she recalls the promise never to forsake her that Christ made to her at her conversion, as related at the beginning of the *Book*. Such specific references to this touching scene, when Margery lies in bed, crazed with grief and guilt, until Christ comes to her, are almost surprising since Margery has long since proved her faithfulness. But the narrative jump is clearly intentional, and it reminds us of the profoundest of medieval beliefs: there can be no rest while we inhabit the earth.

In *Women's Autobiography*, Estelle Jelenik claims that "In the *Book of Margery Kempe* the emphasis [is] on both the hostile and friendly people Kempe met on her pilgrimage, rather than on her religious progress."[57] Such a simplification disregards the penitential patterns and program of *imitatio* that Margery conveys in her narrative, in which the active and contemplative lives are inseparably bound in accordance with the Franciscan tradition. Jelenik is right, however, to probe the "multidimensionality" of Margery's role and connect this element to the fragmented, diffuse nature of her autobiography.[58] Ultimately the autobiography is a study of her ambiguous role as an effective Christian and layperson in a society where her gender deprives her of the authority to impart what she had learned from the devotions intended by the Franciscans to enlighten laypersons. Her book fluctuates between biographical and hagiographical structures, reflecting her search for spiritual and psychological wholeness and the struggle against the fragmentation that her society simply accepted as woman's plight. Because she is a layperson, and not an anchoress like Julian, who has a religious identity and can say "I," Margery reverts to third

[56] Atkinson, *Mystic and Pilgrim*, p. 212.

[57] Estelle C. Jelenik, *Women's Autobiography*, p. 8. Also see Fries, "Margery Kempe," pp. 217–37. Fries notes, in contrast: "The *Book* has been accused of lacking form . . . but whether consciously or not, Margery introduced a pattern, sometimes chronological despite her disclaimer, sometimes associational, that can be discerned once the the book is carefully outlined in a structural rather than chronological fashion. In both Book I and Book II, the key event is conversion" (p. 218).

[58] Jelenik, *Women's Autobiography*, p. 17.

person, distancing and objectifying her experiences. If her own identity is a constant source of bafflement, however, the *Book* makes clear that wholeness comes with conversion. Margery can care for her neighbors, and thus truly imitate Christ, only after she has developed an intimate relationship with him.

With Margery's spiritual health comes a return to sanity. Her conversion unites her tormented mind and self-mutilated body. Like Francis, Margery cares for the poor and sick, whose sense of alienation and isolation she understands. She exercises her humility by extending comfort to those whom medieval society often brutally cast out. Margery's desire to kiss and minister to the lepers, the most pitiful and rejected figures in medieval culture, reminds us of Francis's conversion.[59] In fact, Margery's account is similar and leads one to wonder whether she may have heard the Middle English translation of Bonaventure's account of the episode in the *South English Legendary* (p. 176, lines 34–36; p. 177, lines 1–4):

> Now gan she to louyn þat sche had most hatyd be-fore-tyme, for þer was no-thyng mor lothful ne mor abhomynabyl to hir whil sche was in þe ȝerys of werldly prosperite þan to seen er beheldyn a laȝer, whom now thorw owr Lordys mercy she desyryd to halsyn & kyssen for þe lofe of Ihesu whan sche had tyme & place conuenyent.

Margery wishes to embrace the lepers and thus through charity to reintegrate them into Christian society. Perhaps the most poignant scene of *imitatio* in Margery's *Book*, however, occurs when Margery has the opportunity to minister to a woman who is "owt hir mende" after delivering a child; this scene is surely a mirror image of Margery's own experience at the beginning of the *Book* (p. 177, line 35). Church law rather insensitively demanded a period of ritualistic "cleansing" of women who had delivered children, during which time they could not receive the sacraments. The anxiety, fear, and sense of social and spiritual isolation this law caused, in addition to the physical exhaustion of childbirth, naturally could result in extreme melancholy.[60] The picture Margery relates recalls her own experience of physical binding and isolation (p. 178, lines 18–24):

[59] Atkinson, *Mystic and Pilgrim*, p. 139.

[60] On the denigration of women in canon law see Erikson, *The Medieval Vision*, pp. 194–197.

Sche roryd & cryid so boþe nyth & day for þe most part þat men wolde not suffyr hir to dwellyn a-mongys hem, sche was so tediows to hem. Þan was sche lad to þe forthest ende of þe town in-to a chambyr þat þe pepil xulde not heryn hir cryin. & þer was sche bowndyn handys and feet wyth chenys of yron þat sche xulde smyten no-body.

Moved by this pitiful spectacle, Margery visits the woman once or twice regularly every day, simply speaking to her. This soothes the frantic mother and comforts her until she is ready to receive purification. Like any Tertiary then, Margery discovers a balance between the active and the contemplative life without taking vows. Both actions and meditations, however, reflect the Franciscan ideal. She meditates "weke by weke & day be day, les þan sche wer occupijd wyth seke folke er ellys wer lettyd wyth oþer nedful occupasyon as was necessary vn-to hir er to hir euyn-crystyn" (p. 214, lines 31–34). Like the apostles after the Pentecost, Margery believes that Christ gave her "grace to vndirstondyn hys wil & parformyn it in werkyng" (p. 248, lines 11–12).

The Presentation of the Child, MS Douce 219, fol. 152ᵛ, by permission of the Bodleian Library, Oxford University.

4

Pearl: Penance Through the Dream Vision

Pearl, composed between 1360 and 1390 in Northwest Midland dialect and extant in a single manuscript (Cotton Nero A.x), remains the
most beautiful and elusive of late medieval dream-visions. On the
simplest or literal level, *Pearl* describes the experience of a man who,
grief-stricken by the death of his daughter, must learn the meaning of
loss and suffering in a divine economy. In this process, he is granted
through grace a vision of his child in a scintillating world that tran-
scends mortality. Here, his daughter, transformed by death into a vessel
of wisdom, attempts to instruct the dreamer in the inscrutable ways of
God. This landscape, in dream-like fashion, evolves into the New
Jerusalem of the *Book of Revelation*, where the Pearl maiden, his
daughter, assumes her sanctified place of honor among the Brides of
Christ. Although the dreamer desperately longs to join her, he is cast
out of the Lamb's Court; and upon awakening from his dream, he
realizes the necessity of conforming his own rebellious will to Christ's.
So vivid are the poem's images, so poignant its emotions, that many
early readers assumed *Pearl* was an actual elegy or autobiography. This
conflation of author and dreamer, while it may seem naive to contemporary critics, raised several useful issues for consideration and interpretation, including the religious status of the author, whether layman

or priest—an issue directly related to the sources for, structure of, and iconography in the poem.

As a spiritual autobiography *Pearl* has long perplexed scholarly readers who seem eager to fit the poem into a late-medieval tradition of contemplative or mystical writings.[1] In many ways the poem invites this assignment: its luminous liturgical imagery, perfectly cyclical form, and frequent allusions to scripture point to a learned author familiar with a late-medieval corpus of allegorical works of spiritual growth and mystical vision, including Bonaventure's *Itinerarium* and Dante's *Vita nuova*.[2] Any possible allusions to the *via activa*, from which the elegists drew fragile evidence to support their interpretations, seem elusive, remote, or peripheral in the poem and set the focus more firmly on strictly spiritual matters. Above all, the theme of purity, neatly binding the poet's works, has suggested an association between the author and a "contemplative" or chaste life of priestly perfection. We might easily assume, as did Sister Mary Madeleva, that "no man . . . would be moved to express with such ardor as one finds in the poem, his personal longing for a condition that he had willingly and irrevocably forgone."[3]

This makes good sense to readers who believe that the dreamer's illumination in the poem culminates in a beatific vision, albeit

---

[1] The dispute over *Pearl*'s meaning is lengthy. Among the early editors and editions favoring an elegiac or autobiographical reading of the poem are Richard Morris, ed., *Early English Alliterative Poems in the West Midland Dialect of the Fourteenth Century*; Pearl: *An English Poem of the Fourteenth Century*, 2d ed., ed. and trans. Sir Israel Gollancz; *The* Pearl: *A Middle English Poem*, ed. Charles Osgood, Jr. Among the critics emphasizing the allegorical nature of the poem, following W. H. Schofield's "The Nature and Fabric of the *Pearl*," *PMLA* 19 (1904): 154–215; and his "Symbolism, Allegory, and Autobiography in the *Pearl*," *PMLA* 24 (1909): 585–675, are Sr. Mary Madeleva, Pearl: *A Study in Spiritual Dryness*; Marie P. Hamilton, "The Meaning of the Middle English *Pearl*," *PMLA* 70 (1955): 805–24. Contemporary critics who address both perspectives are E. V. Gordon in his edition of *Pearl*; A. C. Spearing in *The* Gawain *Poet: A Critical Study*; and "Symbolic and Dramatic Development in the *Pearl*," *MP* 60 (1962): 1–12; Patricia Kean, *The* Pearl: *An Interpretation*; Ian Bishop, Pearl *in Its Setting*. For a summary of *Pearl* studies see René Wellek, "*The Pearl*: An Interpretation of the Middle English Poem," in Robert J. Blanch, ed., *Sir Gawain and* Pearl: *Critical Essays*, pp. 3–36.

[2] See Barbara Nolan, *The Gothic Visionary Perspective*, chap. 4, "The Later Medieval Spiritual Quests," pp. 124–55.

[3] Madeleva, *Pearl*, p. 12.

vicariously through the *Book of Revelation*. Indeed, there is no question that "mystical" or "unitive" experiences were considered outside the realm of possibility for an "active" or layperson in the poet's day; its prerequisite was a holy life of contemplation. In chapter 9 of *The Ladder of Perfection*, one of the most influential books of spiritual guidance in the latter part of the fourteenth century, Walter Hilton claims with assurance:

> God gives this degree of contemplation where he will, both to learned and to simple, to men and women in spiritual authority and to solitaries; but it is an especial favor, and not common. And although a person living the active life may receive this gift as an especial favor, none but a contemplative or solitary can possess it in all its fulness.[4]

If the dreamer is a contemplative, therefore, relating spiritual experience in the guise of allegory, his painful struggle toward an ineffable God would end with a rare and blissful encounter comparable to Julian of Norwich's *Revelations*. But the poem's final, solemn stanza tells us that this is not so.

The dreamer's journey and his curiously objective vision of the New Jerusalem, resulting in his denial of a unitive experience, can best be examined within the context of another late-medieval religious tradition — affective devotion — and specifically in relation to the penitential practice of visual meditation. Visual meditation enabled the medieval layperson to explore individual redemption, beginning with penance, in the continuum of God's revelations manifested through time, hence in scripture. In late-medieval conversion literature the sinner discovers the omnipotence of God's will that created humanity to conform eagerly to divine desires through reciprocal love. Christocentric meditation reflects the late-medieval devotional emphasis on Christ's exemplary love as a perfect acceptance of God's will. All these elements are to be found in affective devotion which, unlike contemplation, depends on sensible images, experience, and emotion for its effect. The purpose of such meditation is moral reformation, for it "helps to destroy grave sins and implants virtues."[5]

---

[4] Walter Hilton, *The Ladder of Perfection*, trans. and ed. Leo Shirley-Price, p. 9.
[5] Ibid., p. 40. For a revealing discussion of the efficacy of meditation for Christ's manhood, see chap. 35, pp. 39–40.

We might initially compare *Pearl* to other works about religious experience that were written around the same period, such as Richard Rolle's *Fire of Love* or Julian of Norwich's *Revelations*. In these religious texts the narrator also pays little attention to his or her own identity, focusing primarily on personal experiences that will educate others in their search for an understanding of their roles as pilgrims on earth. Similarly, the didactic note at the end of *Pearl* informs us that the poem's function is not simply to evoke wonder but to instruct others (lines 1201–1204):

> To pay þe Prince oþer sete saȝte
> Hit is ful eþe to þe god Krystyin;
> For I haf founden hym, boþe day and naȝte,
> A God, a Lorde, a frende ful fyin.

While the dreamer claims that it is "eþe" to please the Lord, his own experiences illustrate that a process of spiritual maturation precedes being a "god Krystyin" (line 1202). The dreamer's final resolution, to conform his will to Christ, to stop seeking "mysterys" and take communal comfort in the sacraments, suggests that *Pearl* is not about the rare vision of a medieval contemplative but is concerned with the *via activa* (line 1194).[6] The dreamer's vision ends not in the mystical bliss of spiritual beatitude but in an affective experience, reflection, and a repentant heart.[7] The poem, therefore, belongs to the widely encompassing tradition of late-medieval penitential literature.

Neither penitential nor popular devotional literature encouraged the spiritually naïve, like the dreamer, to strive for contemplative experiences.[8] Contemplation was a practice belonging to an advanced

---

[6] See F. E. Richardson, "*The Pearl*: A Poem and Its Audience," *Neophil* 46 (1962): 308–16. Richardson claims that the subject of the poem is salvation and that consequently "there is no need to suppose a limited audience: a lay or mixed one is equally possible" (p. 315). He also notes that the "language of the doctrinal parts is simple enough for any lay audience" and dependent primarily on a "familiarity with the Bible such as any layman could acquire through joining in the services of Church" (p. 315).

[7] Spearing, *The Gawain Poet*, p. 170.

[8] Joseph E. Milosh, The Scale [Ladder] of Perfection *and the English Mystical Tradition*, p. 27. Milosh explains that Hilton, unlike the church fathers, does not view the active life as a prerequisite for the contemplative life: "For Hilton, the active life is a necessity only when worldly cares or God's appointment make it so. Otherwise it is inferior to the contemplative life. Usually the active can hope to attain only 'the lower

stage of spiritual growth and was a special discipline for the clergy, the enclosed, and those mendicants who led both active and contemplative lives. Meditation, rather, accompanied by prayer, was encouraged for the spiritually simple for its "affective and moral uses."[9] If we are familiar with the devotional instruction of the laity, the elaborate programs of spiritual training that emerged from thirteenth- and fourteenth-century evangelism and the penitential tradition, the claims of respected critics that *Pearl* is a unitive vision seem dubious.[10]

In *Pearl* solitary human grief is the catalyst for spiritual vision and meditation; its purpose is to discover the reason for human suffering in God's plan. As a reflective work about one Christian's conversion, *Pearl* dramatizes the transformation of passive suffering into an acceptance, however reluctant, of God's will. Like the simplest penitential lyrics, the poem is (1) experiential, (2) self-examining, (3) dialogic, and (4) affective. It does not examine the triune nature of God, the nature of the soul, or the nature of evil, as do contemplative and mystical works like Julian's *Revelations*. Its end is penance and an embracing of those sacraments which serve as exemplars pointing to a divinity that must remain veiled to human vision. Like other meditative works, such as Margery's *Book* or the gospel harmonies, scripture in *Pearl* serves as the final authority which gives meanings and patterns to all human experience and history. It is not only elucidated in the *Pearl* maiden's sermon on grace, which adapts the Gospel of Matthew's Parable of the Vineyard, but is incorporated into the text of the poem itself. The *Book*

---

degree of the second part of Christian contemplation,' or fervent prayer and a 'little tasting of the sweetness of the love of God' (*Scale* [*Ladder*] I, vi [p. iv])." In other words, contemplation is a gift of grace, and one cannot receive this gift by merit. What the active can achieve, however, the "higher stage of the second degree" in Hilton's *Ladder*, is "peace of heart and purity of conscience" from "meditation on our Lord. The thought of the Blessed Name of Jesus brings them comfort and joy, and meditation on it feeds their love for Him." See chap. 7 of Hilton, *The Ladder of Perfection*.

[9] In her contextual study of medieval meditative texts Salter repeatedly emphasizes that meditation was a preliminary to mystical contemplation only among these specialized groups. For laypersons meditation served a purely didactic purpose. See Salter, *Nicholas Love's* Myrrour, p. 178. Also see Richard Kieckhefer, *Unquiet Souls*, chap. 4, "Devotion to the Passion," pp. 89–121.

[10] A systematic analysis of the contemplative ascent to unity can be found in Louis Blenkner, "The Theological Structure of *Pearl*," *Traditio* 24 (1968): 43–75; reprinted in John Conley, ed., *The Middle English* Pearl: *Critical Essays*, pp. 220–71.

of Revelation is the final focus of the dreamer's meditations; as in the meditative gospel harmonies of the late Middle Ages, he is invited to "behold" the culmination of God's eschatological plan for humanity.[11] The dreamer observes this mystical text, re-created by the *Pearl* author to transform the scriptural scene from a static image into a living scene, but he cannot enter into it.[12] He can only respond affectively to the pathos of the wounded lamb, for the rest is beyond his understanding. In emphasizing the importance of meditation on the humanity of Christ for the "imperfect," or noncontemplative, the *Meditations on the Life of Christ* claims:

> One is not worthy of being seen until one is worthy of seeing. But when, by living in the hollowed earth, he has accomplished so much in the healing of the inner eye that he may look on the glory of God with his face raised, then he who sees will speak confidently and with pleasing face of. . . those things that he can understand in the light of God. Nor could he see the same thing if he were not clear and pure and thus transformed into the same image of clarity that he sees. Otherwise, because of unlikeness, he would turn back, rejected by an unaccustomed splendor.[13]

The author of the *Meditations* concludes:

> You see how necessary is the meditation on the life of Christ, since by this authority it is shown that if you are not purified you will never be able to reach the most supreme things of God.[14]

[11] For an example of visual practices in meditative texts, see *Meditations on the Supper of Our Lord*, ed. J. Meadows Cooper, p. 35: "Thenk man, and se cryst aftyr hys deþ" (line 1121).

[12] Marie Borroff, "*Pearl*'s 'Maynful Mone': Crux, Simile, and Structure," in Carruthers and Kirk, eds., *Acts of Interpretation*, p. 159.

[13] *Meditations on the Life of Christ*, trans. and ed. Ragusa and Green, p. 262. The Latin reads: "Non erit digna videri, quamdiu non erit idonea videre. Cum autem per inhabitationem fossae humi in sanando oculo interiori tantum profecerit, ut revelata facie speculari gloriam Dei et ipsa possit; tunc demum quae videbit, fiducialiter jam loquitur, voce et facie placens. Placeat necesse est facies, quae in Dei claritatem intendere potest. Neque illud enim posset, nisi clara quoque esset et pura: utique transformata in eamdem, quam conspicit, claritatis imaginem, alioquin ipsa dissimilitudine resilieret, insolito reverberata fulgore." *Meditationes*, ed. Peltier, chap. 1, p. 576.

[14] *Meditations on the Life of Christ*, trans. and ed. Ragusa and Green, p. 262. The Latin reads: "Vides quam necessaria sit tibi vitae Christi meditatio: nam ut ex auctoritate patet, nisi in ea depureris, nunquam ad siblimia Dei ascendere poteris." *Meditationes*, ed. Peltier, chap. 1, p. 576.

In the late-medieval devotional tradition, contemplation on the celestial court and the majesty of God is thus reserved for those who are already pure in faith, according to the Franciscan author of the *Meditations*.[15] In contrast, the *Pearl* dreamer is rebellious to the very end, suggesting that he has yet to heal his "inner eye" (*oculo interiori*) through penance.[16] He has not accepted his plight of living on the "hollowed earth" (*fossae humi*)—his own mortality.[17] The *Pearl* maiden's "catechetical" office is to help the dreamer do so.[18] She is the "personalizing referent" in the poem's eschatological framework. David Jeffrey notes the fundamental importance of such additions in the Franciscan teaching of biblical narrative; familiar, beloved, the maiden becomes the means by which we measure the dreamer's spiritual progress, and thus his transition from earthly to spiritual values.[19]

While acknowledging the meditative process, and thus the movement toward penance in the narrative of *Pearl*, we also find it useful and even necessary to identify the poem's literary typology, for it created certain expectations in medieval listeners and readers. *Pearl* is, first, a *visio spirituale*, a meaningful dream in which spiritual truths are embodied as sensory images pressed upon the imagination.[20] Like the English mystics, who put their language into the difficult service of objectifying highly individualistic experiences, the *Pearl* poet necessarily turns to the language of sensory experience to illustrate the dreamer's singular journey toward God.[21] At times the narrator ques-

[15] *Meditations on the Life of Christ*, trans. and ed. Ragusa and Green, p. 260. The Latin reads: "Scire autem debes contemplationis tria esse genera: duo principalia propter perfectos; tertium additur pro imperfectis. Duo perfectorum sunt contemplatio majestatis Dei, et contemplatio coelestis curiae. Tertium pro incipientibus et imperfectis est contemplatio humanitatis Christi, quam in hoc libello tibi describo." *Meditationes*, ed. Peltier, chap. 1, p. 576.

[16] *Meditations on the Life of Christ*, ed. Ragusa and Green, p. 262.

[17] Ibid.

[18] Braswell, *The Medieval Sinner*, p. 95. Braswell discusses *Pearl*'s borrowings from a penitential literary tradition in chap. 3, "Confession as Characterization in the Literature of Fourteenth-Century England," pp. 61–101.

[19] Jeffrey, *The Early English Lyric*, p. 48. Jeffrey defines this as a "vernacular literary tool" in which interpolating, i.e., dramatizing, creating roles or commentators, serves the "psychological function" of elucidating or sharpening the practical spiritual application of biblical narrative. This is certainly the *Pearl* maiden's purpose in the poem.

[20] Theodore Bogdanos, *Pearl: Image of the Ineffable*, p. 37.

[21] For a brief introduction of the problematic and creative aspects of English

tions this process, which reflects, perhaps, the poet's frustration with the limitations of language. Even in the *visio* — the earthly paradise that is a reflection of our mutable world — the dreamer finds himself lacking a vocabulary with which to convey his vision and emotions (lines 133–36):

> More of wele watʒ in pat wyse
> Þen I cowþe telle þaʒ I tom hade,
> For vrþely herte myʒt not suffyse
> To þe tenþe dole of þo gladneʒ glade.

Like visual meditation, poetry necessarily incarnates ideas or feelings that are difficult to express; both consequently rely on a verbal and visual iconography that is largely associative. The medieval listener was highly responsive to this pool of images from which spiritual and secular writers drew. In an analysis of the evocative nature of the medieval religious lyric, V. A. Kolve says that "words become pictures, pictures give birth to words. In the Middle Ages, to be an audience to an image (whether verbal or visual) implied activity, not passivity. It called one to thought, to feeling, to meditation."[22]

Pearl's iconography derives from literary works as varied as the *Roman de la Rose* and the mystical *Song of Songs*.[23] Both mesh the spiritual and psychological workings of humankind, appealing to felt experience through metaphor; they give a visual landscape to emotional states and a geography to the uncharted territories of the human psyche. The poem's posture as a "dream" merely informs the reader that the narrator has entered the domain of the imagination. Whether the poet refers to literal sleep or to a spiritual "sleep" that became a metaphor for the occasion of spiritual enlightenment, revelation, and grace in the works of the mystics is immaterial.[24] The boundaries

---

mystical prose, see Wolfgang Riehle, *The Middle English Mystics*, trans. Bernard Standring, intro., pp. 1–13.

[22] V. A. Kolve, *Chaucer and the Imagery of Narrative*, p. 30.

[23] Kean, *The Pearl*, p. 16. Riehle's summary of the influence of the metaphorical language of the Song of Songs on widely known fourteenth-century English mystical writings is also helpful; see *The Middle English Mystics*, pp. 2–5.

[24] Riehle, *The Middle English Mystics*, chap. 10, "The Mystical Experience of God as Rest, Sleep, Death, and Complete Absorption of the Self," pp. 134–47, provides fascinating parallels to the phenomenon of late-medieval dream poetry.

between worldly, waking experience and spiritual experience are intentionally blurred as an indication of their interdependence; for "spirituality, even more than love, has always spoken a symbolic language,
and without parable its speech almost does not exist."[25]

Those great creators and teachers of parables, the Franciscans, rather
than denying the usefulness of images in expressing the divine, fostered a body of literature that depended heavily on the incarnation of
spiritual metaphors.[26] In addition to the journey motif, the Bonaventuran ascent toward the Godhead, with its Augustinian, tripartite
structure, has apparently provided the conceptual form for the order of
events in *Pearl*, according to some readers. Louis Blenkner's examination of the tripartite narrative structure of *Pearl*, for example, concludes
that it is indeed patterned directly after the *Itinerarium*.[27] Like the
Itinerarium, *Pearl* is a "carefully structured, poetic account of a spiritual
itinerary" or an "interior drama" resulting in "psychic change."[28]
Plagued by a world weariness similar to the *Pearl* dreamer's, Bonaventure fled to Alverna seeking rest and spiritual peace. In the mountain's
solitude he experienced a mystical union with God. Blenkner, however,
presses the analogy too far, for, while he is correct in comparing
Bonaventure's threefold path "from without to within to above" to the
narrative movement of *Pearl*, he believes that the poem "culminated in
an ecstasy of mystical contemplation" like the *Itinerarium*.[29] He notes
that Bonaventure's source, Hugh of Saint Victor, describes this pattern
as "cogitation, meditation, and contemplation" or consideration of
"the created, the literal (Scripture or human history) and the
Eternal."[30]

The poem's focus on purgation and scripture, however, indicates
that this analogy halts after the meditative and literal stages, since the
dreamer is unprepared to receive a fuller vision, which occurs in a
human lifetime only through an extreme act of grace or after death. No

---

[25] Madeleva, *Pearl*, p. 89.
[26] Fleming, *An Introduction to the Franciscan Literature of the Middle Ages*,
p. 251.
[27] Blenkner, *The Middle English Pearl*, p. 242.
[28] Ibid., p. 221.
[29] Ibid.
[30] Ibid., p. 227.

doubt the poet borrows from the affective love language of mystical experience to emphasize the dreamer's illumination.[31] Words like *langour, rauvyst, longeyng,* and *swone* (lines 357, 1088, 244, 1180), however, belong to a shared vocabulary of courtly and mystical writers and do not suggest that the dreamer's "veray avysyoun" is the transcendent falling asleep on the cross in darkness that Bonaventure describes: "Let us say with Dionysius 'But you, my friend, concerning mystical visions, with your journey more firmly determined leave behind your senses and intellectual activities and sensible and invisible things.'"[32]

Bonaventure is speaking of complete integration into the Godhead, or a kind of spiritual unity that is impossible for the dreamer. At the end of the poem his inability to leave his "lyttel quene" in her company of maidens reminds us that he has yet to amend his willfulness. Like the reader, who is far more comfortable in the languishing garden at the opening of the poem than in the bright monotony of this transcendent world, the dreamer longs for that which is familiar to him.

According to Hugh of Saint Victor, meditation upon the familiar, through the sensible world or through revelation in historical time (scripture), is the only way a believer can discover moral imperatives in the fallen world:

> In meditation the mind makes an effort to discover the divine, though hidden beneath the veil of sensible images or the surface of holy writings. The truth is presented to us, imprisoned as it were, in the sensible and enveloped in darkness — we must free it and bring it fully to light. This results from the meditative effort of the soul. It is thus we learn what God commands us to do. But before we reach contemplation it is necessary that we should conform our life to the teachings discovered in meditation.[33]

---

[31] Riehle, *The Middle English Mystics,* chap. 3, "The Song of Songs and Metaphors for Love in English Mysticism," pp. 34–55.

[32] Bonaventure, *The Soul's Journey into God,* trans. and ed. Cousins, p. 114–15. The Latin reads: "...cum Dionysio.... Ad amicum autem, cui haec scribuntur, dicatur cum eodem: 'Tu autem, o amice, circa mysticas visiones corroborati itinere, et sensus desere et intellectuales operationes et sensibilia et invisibilia et omne non ens et ens, et ad unitatem, ut possibile est, inscius restituere ipsius.'" Bonaventure, *Itinerarium,* chap. 7, no. 5, p. 313.

[33] Pourrat, *Christian Spirituality,* p. 118. See his discussion of "Intuitive Meditation" and Hugh of St. Victor's "De modo dicendi et meditandi; De meditando seu meditandi artificio," pp. 117–20.

The prerequisite for contemplation or for any deeper spiritual experience is moral reformation. The key to the poem's abrupt ending lies in the dreamer's inability to pass beyond the purgative stage, with which the poet is primarily concerned. While the dreamer may meditate on the celestial vision of the New Jerusalem, he cannot have a "mystical" or unitive experience.[34] For the patient believer sufficient consolation is provided on earth through the sacraments and scripture. As the *Pearl* maiden repeatedly emphasizes to the curious dreamer, Christ is the mediator and human exemplar and thus humanity's only real assurance of eternal life (lines 649–52):

> "Innoghe þer wax out of þat welle,
> Blod and water of brode wounde.
> Þe blod vus boȝt fro bale of helle
> And delyuered vus of þe deth secounde."

It might be argued that this poem of all the late-medieval lyrics and dream visions is less pointedly Christocentric and thus least representative of a Franciscan visual aesthetic. It is true that there are few direct allusions to the Crucifixion in the poem, nor do we have the dramatic tableaux of the meditative lyrics. The shifting symbolism of the pearl, the lamb, and the Eucharist, however, are profoundly Christocentric. In assuming these various, familiar guises, the poem's imagery leads us to the heart of the mystery of Incarnation: all created things point explicitly to Christ:

> For every creature is by its nature a kind of effigy and likeness of the eternal wisdom, but especially one which in the book of Scripture has been elevated through the spirit of prophecy to prefigure spiritual things . . . and most especially, a creature which God willed to institute as a symbol and which has the character not only of a sign in the general sense but also of a sacrament.[35]

[34] Kean, *The Pearl*, p. 231.
[35] Bonaventure, *The Soul's Journey into God*, trans. and ed. Cousins, p. 77. The Latin reads: "Omnis enim creatura ex natura est illius aeternae sapientiae quaedum effigies et similitudo, sed specialiter illa quae in libro Scripturae per spiritum prophetiae assumta est ad spiritualium praefigurationen, specialius autem illae creaturae, in quarum effigie Deus angelico ministerio voluit apparere, specialissime vero ea quam voluit ad significandum institutere, quae tenet non solum rationem signi secundum nomen commune, verum etiam sacramenti." Bonaventure, *Itinerarium*, chap. 2, no. 12, p. 303.

Franciscan exegetes, ever with an eye toward the necessity of *imitatio* or perfect moral transformation, focused on the "letter" of the text or its "spiritual principles" (*moraliter*).[36] The primary purpose of scripture was to illustrate how one might conform to Christian moral principles both in the heart and externally through a manner of living. As a symbol of the word made flesh, Christ instituted a pattern of living to which all Christians must adhere before they can further comprehend the meaning of spiritual signs (tropological, allegorical, anagogical).

In the early seventeenth century Sir Robert Cotton's librarian described *Pearl* as "An old English poem in which, under the fiction of a dream, many things concerning religion and morals are explained."[37] *Pearl*'s first critic interpreted the poem's chief purpose as being to convey moral truths. That is not surprising when we consider that scriptural paraphrase is the warp and woof of the poem. Also the maiden's sermonizing consists largely of scriptural explication with the intent of producing a moral transformation in the dreamer. *Pearl* functions on the same principle of slow spiritual awakening that we see in Bonaventure's biography of Francis. Through dreams, meditations, and visions Francis achieved a moral reformation that led to the mystical, symbolic experience of the stigmata. Throughout his life, however, Francis was drawn to mystical symbols, like the tau, from which emanate a mysterious sense of the invisible source of all good. Theodore Bogdanos identifies the same incarnational ethos in *Pearl*:

> Furthermore, the symbolic significance of each creature is part of its nature, built into it by God rather than invented by man. Franciscan spirituality and its aesthetics, as well as its emotionalism and its appeal to earthbound, familiar experience, increase the impact of the symbolic surface in any poetic context. Without committing the excesses of the late middle ages, *Pearl* shares this temper; it has its own *gloria passionis*.[38]

Like the early Franciscan lyrics or *laudes*, *Pearl*'s third stanza reflects a

36 Jeffrey, *The Early English Lyric*, p. 86. For my discussion of Franciscan exegesis, I am indebted to Jeffrey's informative exposition on pp. 85–95.

37 Conley, *The Middle English Pearl*, intro., p. vii. The Latin original reads: "vetus poema Anglicanum, in quo sub insomni figmento multa ad religionem et mores spectantia explicantur." Ibid.

38 Bogdanos, *Pearl*, p. 8. On pp. 6–9 Bogdanos briefly surveys the development of medieval symbolist thought, including the contributions of Bonaventure and Hugh of St. Victor.

sensitivity to the harmonious beauty of the created world, painstakingly shaped by the Master Craftsman who is so prominent a figure in Franciscan theology.[39] The garden's bright flowers and autumnal ripeness point to the cyclical process of death and regeneration that becomes the primary metaphor for spiritual resurrection in *Pearl*.[40] Seeing the earth's fecundity replenished through death and decay, the dreamer mournfully echoes the most optimistic belief of Christianity: "of goud vche goud is ay bygonne" (line 33). God is himself the highest good, and it is his nature to be "self-diffusive."[41] All that he creates, therefore, reflects this property, including the inscrutable scheme of death and rebirth.

In the mystical literature of fourteenth-century England, the word "siȝt" is often linked with understanding or "cnawyng," and thus verbally associates spiritual knowing with visionary experience.[42] Among the many sources of this association is Augustine's belief that "the eyes are the chief of our senses for acquiring knowledge."[43] The dreamer, having observed the patterns of creation, is aware that his destiny is hinted at through earthly vestiges of God — "reflections of glory projected into the obscure depths of the void."[44]

As an example of medieval faith in a divine economy, we have Francis's own jubilant "Canticle of the Sun," which benevolently personifies "Sister Bodily Death" as a necessary figure in God's intricately balanced world.[45] In contrast, the dreamer's response to the mortality of the "erber" is melancholic. While he recognizes the vestiges of a

---

[39] Bonaventure, *Works*, trans. and ed. Ewart Cousins, p. 74. The Augustinian origins of this concept and its prominence in late-medieval poetry are acknowledged by Alfred L. Kellogg in "Pearl and the Augustinian Doctrine of Creation," in Conley, ed., *The Middle English Pearl*, pp. 335–37. Also see Jeffrey, *The Early English Lyric*, chap. 2, "Aesthetics and Spirituality."

[40] Edward Vasta, "*Pearl*: Immortal Flowers and the Pearl's Decay," in Conley, ed., *The Middle English Pearl*, pp. 185–202. Vasta locates the major themes of the poem in the third stanza and addresses varying critical interpretations.

[41] Bonaventure, *Itinerarium*, chap. 6, no. 2.

[42] Riehle, *The Middle English Mystics*, p. 123. Riehle surveys the development of sight as a mystical metaphor in chap. 8, "The Experience of God as a Spiritual Sense Perception," pp. 122–27.

[43] Augustine, *The Confessions*, trans. Sir Tobie Matthew, p. 310.

[44] Gilson, *The Philosophy of St. Bonaventure*, p. 168.

[45] Bonaventure, *Works*, ed. Cousins, p. 28.

divinely ordered nature in the garden, he derives no hope from the certainty that "vche gresse mot grow of grayneʒ ded" (line 31). In his grief over the human condition, mortality can be translated only into faithless and shortsighted terms of deprivation. This attitude illustrates the dreamer's willfulness and prepares the reader as early as the fifth stanza of the poem for the spiritual drama of conversion and penance. It also suggests, however, that Everyman's vision is limited, or skewed by sin. It comes as no surprise, later in the poem, that the dreamer and the *Pearl* maiden dispute over varying perceptions stemming from their earthly and heavenly stances.

From the beginning the poet stresses that humankind's intellectual faculties, "resoun" alone, cannot provide the comforting knowledge of spiritual regeneration beyond empirical proof. The dreamer must have faith before he, like Francis, can interpret those vestiges of God's order in nature. As the poem will reveal, this faith is always a result of grace:

> The fact is that human reason alone is incapable of directing itself aright without the help of a superior influence; it has not in itself the power to set its own resources in action; revelation alone saves it from false paths, directs its course, and leads it to its true goal. Reason is only fully itself when it operates in the light of revelation.[46]

In the framework of Christian eschatology, this revelation that redeems all time is the incarnation of Christ. Although the dreamer has been taught that the Incarnation, or "kynde of Christ" (line 55), the "exemplar" and visible proof of God's love, is his comfort, his own willfulness prevents him from fully accepting this as consolation for his private sorrow. Thus the dreamer's desperate reasoning in stanza 3 — "so semly a sede moʒt fayly not" (line 34) — lacks conviction. He still pictures his *Pearl* "spenned" or imprisoned in a clay grave, rather than transformed or resurrected through death (line 53). To medieval man this was indeed a grim picture of death without resurrection, painted frequently in medieval lyrics and sermons.[47] In turn, this bleak image implies that the dreamer is himself "spenned" or imprisoned in the garden, for without faith in the afterlife of his *Pearl* his own existence becomes one futile, linear voyage ending in death. The poem is a

---

[46] Gilson, *The Philosophy of St. Bonaventure*, p. 168.
[47] Gray, *Themes and Images in the Medieval English Religious Lyric*, chap. 10, "Death and the Last Things," pp. 176–221.

meditative quest that explores the various ways humanity can know God and thus be assured of the possibility of salvation. As in all other meditations, the poem turns to the "Bok" that provides a map of God's salvational scheme (line 710).

It is true that the dreamer does not initiate this search or consciously recollect images that will arouse compunction of heart. The poem is a dream vision rather than a prayerful meditation, and it adopts the conventions of its genre. The dream vision, like visual meditation, is nondiscursive and seeks truth through associative experience. The dream vision is thus very much like the episodic meditations we see in Margery's *Book* through which she acquires knowledge and wisdom. Although they stem from a richly productive, visual imagination, Margery's meditations lend her an experiential authority and thus become events that actually seem to have happened. Both the religious dream vision and these narratively complex meditations depend heavily on a highly symbolic imagery, and both, we must remember, were viewed by medieval people as gifts of grace. Although the image-making process of Franciscan meditation was fully conscious, "even the most basic meditation in which a man regards his sins and asks mercy for them, is itself caused by grace put in men's hearts by God."[48] Thus the dreamer emphasizes that his "goste is gon in Godeʒ grace" (line 63).

To stress that the dream vision is a religious vision, the author intentionally draws on a firmly established vocabulary of spiritual experience. The term "slepyng-slaʒte" in the fifth stanza (line 59) recalls the motif of mystical sleep. This is a metaphor for the interior state that can occur in sleep, dream, meditation, or prayer, signifying the awakening of the soul "so that it can understand the processes of its

---

[48] Milosh, *The Scale [Ladder] of Perfection*, p. 79–89. Milosh's discussion of the doctrine of grace is particularly pertinent to readers of *Pearl*. Written ca. 1375, Hilton's writings were known as orthodox works of Christian devotion in Margery Kempe's day (see Kempe, *Book*, chap. 17). The perplexity over a definition of grace pervades *Pearl* and *The Ladder of Perfection*, which share a consistent and orthodox view with Kempe, Julian of Norwich, and the *Cloud* author: "It is true that 'Deus dilectio est,' but it is also true that most important for the progress of the soul is that God gives his love, that is, that God bridges the gulf between the infinite and the finite which man cannot bridge and that God does it freely, since man's efforts can never be great enough to merit God's actions" (Milosh, *The Scale of Perfection*, p. 78).

innermost self and can comprehend divine reality."[49] It is, therefore, the most proper state for activity of the *visio imaginativa*, which Wolfgang Riehle succinctly describes in this way: "In spiritual vision the physical eye and, within, the natural perceptive facilities, are switched off, so that vision occurs in sleep or in prayer and takes the form of man being transplanted to a spiritual seeing."[50]

The dreamer, like Margery Kempe, sees with a "ghostly" eye, or what is frequently described as the "eye of the heart."[51] At least, that is what we initially believe to have happened to the dreamer. But the poet thwarts his audience's expectations, thus creating dramatic tension, by making his dreamer exasperatingly literal-minded. The visionary climate into which the dreamer is thrust proves to be more frustrating than clarifying to him (though not to the audience); while it elusively promises to disclose spiritual mysteries, the vision remains encoded in a symbolic mystical text. The persuasive power of the dream vision ultimately depends less on the dreamer's experiences, in contrast to the final, pessimistic vision in *Piers Plowman*, than on the authority of the *Book of Revelation* as a signpost of God's plan. Throughout the poem the dreamer sees with the limited perspective of an eye erroneously subject first to human reason and thus produces simplistic, empirical deductions from his glorious vision. If we find the end of *Pearl* anticlimactic, the dreamer merely resigned, rather than joyous, we are reponding appropriately to the poem's clearest message: Because of original sin, our vision and reason are clouded. It is our lot to know God "in part," or metaphorically speaking, "through a mirror dimly."[52] We can never see God with our mind's eye, limited as we are by earthbound language and imagination.

In the Earthly Paradise sequence the poet clearly distinguishes between spiritual and physical sight and reminds us of the inadequacy of a language based on the latter to express the serenity of this other world's perfection (lines 97–100):

> So al watȝ dubbet on dere asyse
> Þat fryth þer fortwne forth me fereȝ.

[49] Riehle, *The Middle English Mystics*, p. 137.
[50] Ibid., p. 125.
[51] Ibid., p. 122.
[52] 1 Cor. 13:12.

> Þe derþe þerof for to deuyse
> Nis no wyȝ worþé þat tonge bereȝ.

In the Earthly Paradise the dreamer seems conscious for the first time of the splendor and utter perfection of God's creation — an exemplarism intensified in its frozen beauty. In contrast to the lush garden, where the dreamer laments the sensuousness of a world that implies death, he is now overwhelmed by the stark but brilliant permanence of this conceptual landscape.

The dreamer necessarily returns to primal earthly analogies to communicate his sense of longing and mystery (lines 113–16):

> In þe founce þer stonden stoneȝ stepe,
> As glente þurȝ glas þat glowed & glyȝt,
> As stremande sterneȝ, quen stroþe-men slepe,
> Staren in welkyn in wynter nyȝt.

This passage is one of the poet's most remarkable, for it encapsulates humanity's compulsion to strive toward a reality beyond experience. While the iconic shape of the reality changes throughout human history, its mythic conventions do not. The sky is the veil, untouchable and impenetrable, behind which the ineffable power moving the universe sits enthroned. It is merely another image for Paul's dark mirror, through which mankind peers dimly to glimpse eternal truth (1 Cor. 13:12).[53]

In this section of the poem the dreamer does indeed face the dilemma of the medieval mystics, who discovered that "human language cannot provide a vision of absolute bliss. It has at its disposal only inadequate superlatives."[54] By analogy the dreamer guesses that he is somewhere near the ineffable, or "paradyȝe" (line 137). He is

---

[53] Paul Piehler eloquently discusses this passage in similar terms in *The Visionary Landscape: A Study in Medieval Allegory*, chap. 8, "Pearl," pp. 149–50.

[54] Johan Huizinga, *The Waning of the Middle Ages*, trans. F. Hopman, p. 221; see chap. 17, "Religious Thought Beyond the Limits of Imagination," pp. 220–25. Huizinga's view of medieval incarnational thought, or symbolism, as a "short circuit of thought" disregarding causality suggests that his perception of its value and method is colored by his own critical values (p. 203). Nonetheless, his discussion is provocative and eloquent: "The world unfolds itself like a vast whole of symbols, like a cathedral of ideas. It is the most richly rhythmical conception of the world, a polyphonous expression of eternal harmony" (p. 202).

compelled by an innate desire to see this farther land of tangible beatitude. The dreamer's spiritual limitations, however, are externalized by the physical boundaries of the dream geography. Hampered from crossing the pools to view greater mysteries, he utters with childish expectancy: "And euer me þoȝt I schulde not wonde / For wo þer weleȝ so wynne wore" (lines 153–54). Of course, having refused to accept the death of his Pearl, the dreamer cannot understand the exclusivity of paradise. We are thus perfectly prepared for the dreamer's obtuse questioning of the *Pearl* maiden when she arrives at the opportune moment.

The poet chooses this intensely emotional reencounter to launch into seven stanzas of medieval *descriptio*, which embellishes the poem but also slows the narrative pace markedly. These stanzas basically guide us through the dreamer's thought processes as he firmly identifies the "faunt" that he believes he recognizes (line 161). I suspect that the poet is preparing us for the colloquy ahead by illustrating how deceptive human reason, unenlightened by revelation, really is. Recognition based solely on physical appearance is deceptive: the key episode in the late-medieval mystery plays that dramatizes Christ's encounter with his few disciples at Emmaeus reminded medieval Christians that believers must "overcome rational doubts" or see with their hearts if they are to recognize Christ risen and transformed.[55] The *Pearl* maiden's mission is to teach the dreamer a new kind of knowledge, based not on what he can see but on what he can know in the context of "hyȝ wordes" (line 819), scripture, or revelation. The dreamer must accept the "tale" of redemption (line 310), or God's truth manifested in human space and time, rather than hold tightly to his own narrow apprehension of truth as experienced in the garden.

It is quite clear to the reader from the beginning that this maiden is royally transformed through the spiritual glory of resurrection. The dreamer, however, does not consider her from an enlightened perspective but identifies her from past experience: "I knew hyr wel, I hade sen hyr ere" (line 164). Scanning her exquisite costume, her ivory skin, the diminutive proportions of her body, the dreamer ignores the maiden's transformed appearance, seeking the familiar in a recognizably human

[55] David Bevington, *Medieval Drama*, p. 628.

way. While overjoyed at beholding her after their separation, the dreamer's response to the maiden is comically inappropriate given her new status. He disregards the fact that the maiden has been resurrected from death and utterly changed; instead, he wonders at seeing her in an unfamiliar place, as if they were friends who happened to meet by chance in a foreign country: "Bot baysment gef myn hert a brunt. / I seʒ hyr in so strange a place" (lines 174–75).

The *Pearl poet*, master of ornate description, sculptures a three-dimensional beauty whom only Dante's Beatrice rivals in her perfection. Yet, like Beatrice, she never assumes a wholly allegorical posture in the poem, for that would destroy the delicate dramatic balance of the spiritual autobiography.[56] The *Pearl* maiden is more like the Blessed Virgin or Saint Mary Magdalene in Margery's meditations than the purely allegorical creation of Lady Philosophy in Boethius's *Consolation*. She is not simply "iconic" but is a complex character, equally familiar and removed, human and idealized. Her voice is memorable and distinct because it addresses the dreamer in a personal rather than purely educative manner. In fact, the dramatic energy of the poem is sustained through the colloquy, in which little actually happens, because of the maiden's familiarity to the dreamer.

In the devotional literature of the late Middle Ages, "perfect" love is usually conceived in human terms. Christocentric devotion centers on humanity's ability to respond to a divine love re-created, out of love, in human forms. Medieval lyrics, therefore, explore Christ's love for mankind using familial relationships.[57] For example, we might consider a fourteenth-century poem to the Virgin by William Herebert (a Franciscan):

> Thou my suster and my moder,
> and thy sone is my brother:

---

[56] Piehler, *The Visionary Landscape*, p. 21, explains that Beatrice's figure is not "based on the figure of a god or goddess, or the closely related figure of the allegorical abstraction...[but] appears in the form of a person encountered in the poet's everyday experience." Piehler writes that in Beatrice Dante established a new type of allegorical figure, balancing the "abstract" with "symbolical and circumstantial feature," a figure whom Piehler also groups with allegorical "figures of history, especially sacred history." The *Pearl* maiden is one of these highly complex allegorical creations.

[57] Gray, *Themes and Images*, pp. 106–21.

Who shulde thenne drede?
Whoso haveth the King to brother,
and ek the quene to moder,
Wel aughte for to spede.[58]

Like such religious lyrics, *Pearl* plays on these spiritual paradoxes by creating a child as mediatrix, who instructs her elder to become a "chylde" and to enter the Kingdom of Heaven (line 723). These lyrics, like the maiden's exposition on grace, suggest that God's love is transforming and uncircumscribed. As an indication of her holy status, the *Pearl* maiden, much to the dreamer's confusion, identifies herself in multidimensional roles. She is a queen, the bride of Christ, and still the least in the kingdom. The dreamer, however, knows only that she was "nerre þen ante or nece" to him (line 233). This phrase does not necessarily serve as evidence of their human relationship but rather informs us that the dreamer is unable to comprehend the transforming power of God's love. Unless he learns to do so, he will neither accept the fact of resurrection after death nor recognize God's extraordinary act of courtesy in joining human and divine natures in Christ.[59]

This section of the poem suggests that mankind can understand holy mysteries only in identifiable ways, as through images, which have physical and spatial properties. And even then, the dreamer, as the *Pearl* maiden points out, does not recognize her at all. In light of her immortality she disclaims the identity that the dreamer assigns to her: she is no longer a rose, encased in a fragile, crumbling shell, but a pearl (line 269-72).

The *Pearl* maiden reproves the dreamer for trusting his vision: "'þou says þou trawez me in þis dene / Bycawse þu may wyth yȝen me se'" (lines 295–96). The passage is a curious one, embedded in a poem that richly cultivates the imagery of medieval religious and romantic quests. *Pearl* was written in an age that demanded tangible proof of its God — in shrines, miracles, and relics. The medieval drama testifies to this hunger for visual reassurance, and the poet's other works, *Patience*, *Purity*, and *Sir Gawain and the Green Knight*, explore the mysterious

---

[58] Davies, ed., *Medieval English Lyrics*, p. 96. For another example of this poetic phenomenon see *A Talkyng of the Love of God*, ed. M. Salvina Westra, p. 28.

[59] Wellek, *The Pearl*, p. 34. "Pearl's symbolism is not simple and cannot be solved by a one-to-one identification with some abstract virtue."

intervention of God in human lives and history to achieve his will. The reader may well ask what is the point of any dream vision if not to prove the divine intervention of God on an individual's behalf. The maiden's argument is a complex one (lines 301–308):

> "I halde þat iueler lyttel to prayse
> Þat leueʒ wel þat he seʒ wyth yʒe,
> And much to blame and vncortayse
> Þat leueʒ oure Lorde wolde make a lyʒe,
> Þat lelly hyʒte your lyf to rayse,
> Þaʒ fortune dyd your flesch to dyʒe.
> ʒe setten hys wordes ful westernays
> Þat leueʒ noþynk bot ʒe hit syʒe."

God's supreme act of unqualified charity, or "courtesy" in the *Pearl* poet's vocabulary, was to allow his son to die and be raised as a sign and a promise ("lelly hyʒte") to redeem all believers.[60] The dreamer's despair over his loss and his inability to see the maiden's transformation implies that he lacks faith. In depending on his "one skyl" instead of revelation, he commits the sin of spiritual pride (line 312). As the *Pearl* maiden tells him, humanity's direct relationship with God was "'forgarte at Paradys greue'" (line 321). His own inheritance is suffering: "Who nedeʒ schal þole, be not so þro" (line 344).

The *Pearl* maiden rightly views the dreamer's stubbornness (he is "þro") as an act of rebellion against God; he has little choice other than to accept her death and separation from him. With her pure perspective she immediately sees that his error lies in making his human love rather than Christ the "'grounde of alle'" his "'blysse'" (line 371). Rather than striving against the Lord, the dreamer must make reparation through "'prayer'" and seek comfort for his loss through "'hys pyte'" (line 355).

In the dialogue that follows, the *Pearl* maiden fruitlessly attempts to instruct the dreamer in the ways of heaven; the paradoxes, however, which are possible in the language of theology, uncircumscribed by physical reality, simply baffle the dreamer. His confusion points once again to the fact that human vision, and hence metaphor, is limited in its power to approximate the ineffable. The exchange between them

---

[60] Kean, *The Pearl*, p. 189.

not only is central to the poem's meaning but illustrates two divergent trends in late-medieval spirituality. On the one hand, late-medieval religiosity is often characterized stylistically by its preoccupation with "rigidifying thought into image."[61] In opposition, and particularly in medieval English spirituality, there is a strong strain of the *via negativa* best exemplified by *The Cloud of Unknowing*, written in the *Pearl* poet's own day.[62] We sense some of the Pearl maiden's exasperation in the following passage from the *Cloud* questioning the potency of the visual imagination in coming to know God:

> & wene not, for I clepe it a derknes or a cloude, þat it be any cloude congelid of þe humo*u*rs þ*a*t fleen in þe ayre, ne ȝit any derknes soche as in þin house on niȝtes, when þi ca*n*del is oute. For soche a derknes & soch*e* a cloud maist þou ymagin wiþ coriouste of witte, for to bere before þin iȝen in þe liȝtest day of somer; & also aȝenswarde in þe derkest niȝt of wynter þou mayst ymagin a clere schinyng liȝt. Lat be soche falsheed; I mene not þus. For when I sey derknes, I mene a lackyng of knowyng; as alle þat þing þ*a*t þou knowest not, or elles þat þou hast forȝetyn, it is derk to þee, for þou seest it not wiþ þi goostly iȝe. & for þis skile it is not clepid a cloud of eire, bot a cloude of unknowyng, þat is bitwix þee & þi God.[63]

"Imagination" here suggests recollection of common, temporal experience, thus deriving from the Latin *imago* that Bonaventure uses in the *Lignum* to discuss imaginative meditation.[64] It refers to an imitation, a picture, a semblance of what is possible or probable in everyday life.[65] The author's reference to such metaphorical thinking as "falsheed," however, suggests that he is making distinctions between substantive realities and imaginatively conjured forms — and all such mental pictures are products of the "witte," or fanciful creations.[66] The

[61] Bogdanos, *Pearl*, p. 117.

[62] For an introduction to the historical and religious context of *The Cloud of Unknowing*, see Walsh, ed., *Pre-Reformation English Spirituality*, pp. 170–81; Knowles, *The English Mystical Tradition*, pp. 57–99.

[63] *The Cloud of Unknowing*, ed. Phyllis Hodgson, p. 23.

[64] Bonaventure, *Works*, ed. Cousins, p. 76.

[65] *OED*, s.v. *Imaginen*, 1: "To form, fashion, to picture oneself, fancy, imagine"; 4: "to ponder, consider, meditate."

[66] *MED*, s.v. *Imaginen*. The verb *imaginen* has two distinct meanings that are applicable here: a. "to form a mental picture of something not present," or to visualize, as perhaps in meditation. According to *MED*, the verb *imagen* (OF *imagier*) is used in this manner primarily in religious texts at early dates, e.g., c. 1390, *Talking of the Love of God* (62; 22); c. 1396, Walter Hilton's *Scale of Perfection* (1.81.55.b). "Imaginen"

author emphasizes that metaphors based on tangible shapes and experience can, at best, hint at a truly spiritual reality.

This does not mean that humankind is wholly deprived of an empirical knowledge of God. The *Pearl* maiden turns to scriptural analogies, such as Saint Paul's comparison of the Church to the body of Christ (lines 457–68), to explain how earthly hierarchies are vestiges of a divine order. Scripture was given to mankind for this purpose and is thus translated into a familiar parabolic language of metaphor and simile (lines 497–500):

> "As Mathew meleʒ in your messe
> In sothfol gospel of God almyʒt,
> In sample he can ful grayþely gesse,
> And lykneʒ hit to heuen lyʒte."

Like the mendicant preachers of the poet's own day, the *Pearl* maiden embellishes the Parable of the Vineyard in her exposition on grace; she relies on the authority of Christ's words to establish her ideas but appeals to the dreamer's sensibilities by depicting the transient world in familiar medieval terms that recall the opening scene of the poem.[67] Once again it is harvesttime, when the laborers toil steadily in the fields until the bell rings the liturgical office of "evensonge" at dusk (line 529).

The dreamer, however, continues to depend on his own feeble reason in an effort to understand God's system of grace and rewards. Limited by a legalistic sense of "desserte" (line 595) rather than God's

---

appears in this context in c. 1400, *Prick of Conscience* (2306) and c. 1440 in Margery Kempe's *Book* (219: 32/30). The other meaning of *imaginen* to which the *Cloud* author refers is "to suppose mistakenly," or fancy (*MED*, p. 83). The issue presented to modern readers is what particular distinctions between fancy and fact in narrative were made by medieval writers and whether perhaps devotional writers considered meditative imaginings to be outside the realm of fancy. The question becomes more clearly defined during the Renaissance, particularly in relation to biographical narratives. For discussions of this issue see Anderson, *Biographical Truth*, and Nelson, *Fact or Fiction*. I myself agree with Clarissa Atkinson, who believes that the distinction was irrelevant in affective devotional writings of the fourteenth century. See Atkinson, *Mystic and Pilgrim*, p. 140: "Most people, who could not read the Bible, knew their religion best through Franciscan stories with emotion and emphasis. The literal story was less important than the penitence it produced; any incident that moved the believer was 'true' in the sense that mattered."

[67] Spearing, *The* Gawain *Poet*, p. 101.

bountiful mercy, the dreamer concludes that, if what the *Pearl* maiden says is true, "'Holy Wryt is bot a fable'" (line 592). Throughout the rest of *Pearl* the poet depends on scriptural paraphrase to illustrate the dreamer's movement from error and unbelief to a spiritual acceptance of God's divine order.[68] At this point it is convenient to recall Hugh of Saint Victor's definition of meditation as a penetration of sensible images, *or the surface of holy writings*, as a means of elucidating the meaning in divine revelations.[69] Central to the *Pearl* maiden's discourse is the importance of scripture as a foundation for the sacraments that guide the medieval Christian on his or her path of holy living (lines 709–12):

> "Ryȝtwysly quo con rede,
> He loke on bok and be awayed
> How Jesus hym welke in areþede,
> And burneȝ her barneȝ vnto hym brayde."

Through her exposition of the Gospels the *Pearl* maiden rebuts the dreamer's belief that grace is a quantifiable gift earned by human beings. Whatever the age or station of the individual, the condition necessary for entering heaven is to be Christlike, or "'wythouten mote oþer mascle of sulpande synne'" (line 726). Innocence is a childlike state, for children "'con not rave'" (line 665). To achieve this state, an adult must be shriven (lines 661–64):

> "Grace innogh þe mon may haue
> Þat synneȝ þenne new, ȝif hym repente,
> But wyth sorȝ and syt he mot hit craue,
> And byde þe payne þerto is bent."

The *Pearl* maiden is alluding to "perfect" penance, or "'contryssyoun'" (line 669).[70] For the dreamer this means that he must approach penance not out of fear, loss, or reason but simply through love. He must repent his willfulness and withstand the pain of human loss as God's more immanent will. The *Pearl* maiden's speech is textured with phrases and images from the penitential literature of the age. Of particular importance is her reference to the wounded lamb: "'In hys

---

[68] Nolan, *The Gothic Visionary Perspective*, p. 193.
[69] Pourrat, *Christian Spirituality*, p. 118.
[70] Tentler, *Sin and Confession*, pp. 24–27.

blod. . . he wesch my wede on dese'" (line 766). This was an especially common image in mystical and penitential writing of the fourteenth century, and, while it explicitly refers to Christ, it prefigures the glorious icon of the apocalyptic lamb that we see at the end of the poem.[71] In its penitential context it is a metaphor for the Passion, which, in Roman Catholic eschatology, assures all human beings of justification. The *Pearl* maiden follows this reference, therefore, with a full explanation of the historical event (lines 805–16):

> "In Jerusalem watȝ my lemman slayn
> And rent on rode wyth boyeȝ bolde.
> Al oure baleȝ to bere ful bayn,
> He toke on hymself oure careȝ colde.
> Wyth boffeteȝ watȝ hys face flayn
> Þat watȝ so fayr on to byhold.
> For synne he set hymself in vayn,
> Þat neuer hade non hymself to wolde.
> For vus he lette hym flyȝe and fold
> And brede vpon a bostwys bem;
> As meke as lomp þat no playnt tolde
> For vus he swalt in Jerusalem."

This passage rivals the most celebrated of medieval passion lyrics, and it certainly intends to produce an affective response. The *Pearl* maiden's ecstatic return of love exemplifies the way in which meditative penitential lyrics functioned as a preparation for perfect penance: "My Lombe, my Lorde, my dere juelle / My joy, my blys, my lemman fre" (lines 795–96).

At the opening of the poem the dreamer describes his own emotional and spiritual state being tormented "for care ful colde" (line 50). Clearly the *Pearl* maiden offers the Crucifixion as the antidote for this anxiety: Christ conquered death to provide hope and reassurance for God's people. The maiden remonstrates with the dreamer for lacking the faith to accept this comfort (lines 857–60):

---

[71] On the powerful image of the wound in popular devotional lyrics, see Gray, *Themes and Images*, p. 34; in Franciscan mysticism, see Riehle, *The Middle English Mystics*, pp. 118, 130: "The range of metaphors for the dialogue between God and Man has been developed still further in Franciscan mysticism. Here the wound of Christ which he received from the lance at the Crucifixion is offered to the soul as a dwelling place" (p. 118).

> "Alþaȝ oure corses in clotteȝ clynge,
> And ȝe remen for rauþe wythouten reste,
> We þurȝoutly hauen cnawyng;
> Of on dethe ful oure hope is drest."

Of course, the dreamer cannot have the same kind of "cnawyng" as the maiden, who has already crossed the streams of paradise and is redeemed by this "'one death.'" But the dreamer has other kinds of assurance. Like the audience of the early-fourteenth century Franciscan gospel harmony *Meditations on the Supper of Our Lord*, he must look to "'holy wryt, or seyntes sermons'" for confirmation of his beliefs.[72] The medieval church encouraged all Catholics to embrace a "wryten" tradition of revelation (line 866). By meditating on these texts, by re-creating or envisioning them, the dreamer can have an experiential "cnawyng" of his individual role in the great scheme the *Pearl* maiden describes as being initiated by Adam's fall "'Þurȝ an apple þat he vpon con byte'" (line 640) and ending with eternal glory in the "'cete of God'" (line 952).

Meditations on the Supper of Our Lord invites the meditator to "Thenk, man, and se Cryst after hys deþ," or to try to envision Christ's descent into hell and the sublimity of the New Jerusalem.[73] In *Pearl* the poet grants his dreamer a vision from the *Book of Revelation* but reminds us throughout that it is not a personal vision but a meditation on a written text. The maiden, wearied by the dreamer's questions, will show him the City of God "'as deuyseȝ hit þe apostel Jhon'" (line 984). Whatever the dreamer sees, he sees "after his tale" (line 985).

The last section of the poem has long puzzled readers. We may be better able to understand the poet's intentions if we consider the devotional tradition with which he was familiar. First, as many critics, including Patricia Kean and Marie Borroff, have noted, the poet, while intentionally paraphrasing sections of the *Book of Revelation*, actually creates a living picture through the principles of selection and emphasis on detail.[74] Knowing what we do about Franciscan meditation, that

[72] *Meditations on the Supper of Our Lord*, ed. Cowper, line 17.
[73] Ibid., line 1121.
[74] On the principles of selection in the description of the Book of Revelation in *Pearl*, see Borroff, "*Pearl*'s 'Maynful Mone,'" p. 159; Bogdanos, *Pearl*, p. 11; Nolan, *The Gothic Visionary Perspective*, pp. 199–200; and Kean, *The Pearl*, pp. 210–24; the last is the most detailed study of this subject.

should not surprise us. Margery Kempe treats large sections of the Gospels in a similar manner, consciously preserving the sound of gospel language and scriptural narrative format as a means of authoritatively buttressing the experience of her meditations with scripture.[75] While Margery's *Book* maintains the sacred and undisputable authority of the gospel text, the focus on particular detail and events informs the reader of Margery's private perspective and interests.

The author of *Pearl* clearly aims to achieve a similar effect; he intentionally gives the impression of translating scripture into English. Again, considering what we know of biblical translations in the fourteenth century, he surely does so to emphasize precisely that this section of the poem *is* meditative, not contemplative. As Margaret Deanesly specifies in her edition of the Lollard Bible, orthodox translations of scripture were paraphrased in the fourteenth century in the gospel harmonies, for meditative, and thus penitential, purposes.[76] This medieval treatment of scripture accords well with the narrative movement in *Pearl*; as yet, the dreamer awaits conversion.

The failure of John's apocalyptic vision to achieve more than conversion disappoints readers, who do, in fact, seem to expect a unitive vision at the end of the poem. Kean, for example, questions the success of the poet in translating the episode from a "distance — almost as a lesson read in church, a retelling, recognizably at some remove, of an impressive and meaningful story."[77] A. C. Spearing finds the rhythmic, liturgical quality of the stanzas, and thus "lack of pressure" in the descriptive technique, a "failing."[78] Interestingly, even Theodore Bogdanos, who recognizes that the poet is not "constructing his own anagogic cosmos" but turning to the authority of scripture, claims, "I do not think we can easily absolve the poet of such an unhappy effect."[79] In contrast, Borroff has noted that the poet's borrowing is an

[75] Kempe, *Book*, pp. 187–94.
[76] Deanesley, *The Lollard Bible*, p. 231. Deanesly notes, as an example, that Richard Rolle's English Psalter "is in several ways characteristic of the attitude of medieval translations. The choice of the book was significant, and shows that the aim was to increase the devotion in those who said the hours and the divine office, and not the general instruction of the laity in the New Testament" (p. 144).
[77] Kean, *The Pearl*, p. 212.
[78] Spearing, *The Gawain Poet*, p. 166.
[79] Bogdanos, *Pearl*, p. 184.

integral and necessary aspect of his artistic enterprise; as in a meditation, the poet uses the *Book of Revelation* as a "transitional image,
standing between a phase of the dream that corresponds with scriptural
authority and a phase of personal experience."[80]

Barbara Nolan, however, explains the poet's impetus for drawing the
final vision more clearly by identifying this part of the poem with
traditions of fourteenth-century piety: "This close meditation on the
word, *a stage of contemplation* proposed by Walter Hilton for those
who seek perfection, is very like the one which the *Pearl* poet finally
offers his readers through the form of the poem" (italics added).[81]
While I am in essential agreement with Nolan, I would argue that the
term "contemplation" lacks precision in reference to the dreamer, who,
as this section of the poem most clearly illustrates, is impervious to
mystical revelation and far from perfection. As proof of this, the
dreamer marvels at the beauty of the New Jerusalem but displays an
earthly joy and sense of possession when he finally sees his daughter.

In this section the poet is no doubt telling us something fundamental about human nature and the spiritual state of his dreamer. For the
dreamer's view of the lamb precedes his recognition of his "lyttel
quene" (line 1147). Inappropriately, it is the maiden, rather than the
wounded lamb, who fills him with "luf-longyng" (line 1151). If we
closely examine the stanza in which the dreamer describes the lamb, it
becomes apparent that his response to this iconic figure of suffering is
primarily "affective." He pities the lamb but never makes the connection between the wounds of the Crucifixion and his own sinful state. In
keeping with his spiritual myopia the dreamer acknowledges what the
proper penitent reaction must be in any human being who sees the
lamb, but he does not so react himself (lines 1135–40):

> Bot a wounde ful wyde and weete con wyse
> Anende hys herte, þurȝ hyde torente.
> Of his quyte syde his blod outsprent.
> Alas, þoȝt I, who did þat spyt?
> Ani brest for bale aȝt haf forbrent
> Er he þerto hade had delyt.

[80] Borroff, *"Pearl's* 'Maynful Mone,'" p. 159.
[81] Nolan, *The Gothic Visionary Perspective*, p. 202.

Like all other sinners, the dreamer "did þat spyt," and he will not make the figurative *transitus* across the river into the New Jersualem until he does repent. Scholars of medieval apocalyptic writing remind us that these panoramic scenes of the Final Judgment reinforced the church's moral teachings, emphasizing that redemption follows only purgation, and in Christian history "this process must be cosmic as well as individual."[82] Consequently, there was a strong didactic strain in most apocalyptic writing in the Middle Ages and a continuous approbation of those who could endure the trial of suffering while waiting.[83] The exotic, often bizarre symbols richly interwoven on the pages of late-medieval apocalypses had a simple subtext: Be "watchful servants," like the laborers in the Parable of the Vineyard.[84]

Apocalyptic spirituality in the late Middle Ages had one other distinguishing characteristic pertinent to the dreamer's anxiety about the death and decay of his Pearl. Apocalyptic texts promised "individual survival after death in the distinctive form of the resurrection of the flesh."[85] Of all the scriptural books, therefore, the *Book of Revelation* is the most fitting for the dreamer's meditations, addressing the questions about the resurrection that he anguishes over in the earthly garden at the very beginning of the poem.

Louis Blenkner, in his generally excellent and eloquent essays on the *Pearl*, states that at the dreamer's vision of the lamb he is filled with a "luf-longyng" for eternal beatitude.[86] Blenkner suggests that "the dreamer's will at this point contemplates the highest good itself, not something that leads to it, or something which has some resemblance to it."[87] The dreamer's own actions, however, contradict this suggestion. If the apostle John comprehended the promise of imminent judgment and redemption of which his vision was the harbinger, the dreamer clearly does not. The vision remains encoded; his "manez

[82] Marjorie Reeves, Introduction, in Bernard McGinn, trans. and ed., *Apocalyptic Spirituality*, p. xiv.

[83] McGinn, trans. and ed., *Apocalyptic Spirituality*, p. 12.

[84] Reeves, Introduction, in ibid., p. xiii.

[85] McGinn, trans. and ed., *Apocalyptic Spirituality*, p. 14.

[86] Blenkner, "The Theological Structure of *Pearl*, in Conley, ed., *The Middle English* Pearl, p. 221.

[87] Ibid., p. 225.

mynde" cannot penetrate the mysteries that he sees (line 1154). In his "rasch and ronk" way the dreamer, who has failed to understand the meaning of physical death in Christian terms, attempts to cross the stream. His desperate intention "to swymme þe remnaunt, þaz I þer swalt" (line 1160) stems from his pathetic desire to remain with his daughter; this he is willing to do, in spite of the starkness of the New Jerusalem and her own strangely transformed, dispassionate nature (line 1160). While the reader certainly sympathizes with the dreamer, his obstinance affirms that he has much preparation to undergo before he can safely "in þe strem astraye" (line 162). As the *Meditations on the Life of Christ* says: "Nor could he (the penitent) see the same thing if he were not clear and pure and thus transformed into the same image of clarity that he sees. Otherwise, because of unlikeness, he would turn back, rejected by an unaccustomed splendor."[88]

Because he is cast out of the visionary realm, the dreamer has learned that, while he inhabits this "doel-doungeon" (line 1187), he has a pattern to follow, or a role to play that, if performed faithfully, will transform him into a "precious perle" (line 1212). Only believers who are Christlike, "homly hyne" (humble servants), wholly submitting their wills to God's, can hope to have the full vision of the redeemed.

[88] *Meditations on the Life of Christ*, trans. and ed. Ragusa and Green, p. 262. The Latin reads: "Neque illud enim posset, nisi clara quoque esset et pura: utique transformata in eamdem, quam conspicit, claritatis imaginem; alioquin ipsa dissimilitudine resiliret, insolito reverberata fulgore." *Meditationes*, ed. Peltier, chap. 1, p. 576.

5

Piers Plowman:
Conversion to Imitation

William Langland's *Piers Plowman* is a spiritual autobiography because it chronicles the conversion of one man's errant will and illustrates how his spiritual reformation reflects change in his waking or external life. As in all other works about spiritual illumination, *Piers Plowman* shows that sin generates chaos and futility whereas conversion results in a personal regeneration and reordering that grants stability to the individual, even in a suffering world. By surmising, as does Donald Howard, that Langland's anxieties are "not personal, but cultural, and in a large measure intellectual," readers of the poem succumb to a dualistic perspective of body divorced from spirit and individual from society against which the poet so vehemently calls for unity.[1] Above all else, *Piers Plowman* asserts that social reformation is impossible without personal reformation beginning in contrition. This interior process, a journey through the self, alone enables men and women to live responsibly in the Christian community. This journey is the "plot" of *Piers Plowman*.[2]

---

[1] Donald Howard, *The Three Temptations: Medieval Man in Search of the World*, p. 165.

[2] See Carruthers, "Time, Apocalypse, and the Plot of *Piers Plowman*."

The purpose of this chapter is to show how the path, in the tradition of affective devotion, inevitably leads to a dramatic or meditative experience of the Incarnation and the Crucifixion. The poem's narrative increasingly insists that we know God experientially — through vision and the symbolic and sacramental realities of everyday life. Thus the poem gradually dissolves the boundaries between dreaming and waking until "symbols become dramatic acts," or "words fully realized in the historical past and, now, in the poem's dreamworld."[3] This unified perception, or clarified vision, is the result of purgation.

Salter has commented, "In some ways the fact that Langland always needed to turn to the drama of flesh and blood was a serious limitation."[4] If we wish to view William the dreamer's role as that of a contemplative and Langland's poem a mystical account of unitive vision, then that is certainly true. I believe, however, that the poet never intended his work to be taken as such, for he constantly pulls us back to the fluctuating, worrisome field of folk where *imitatio*, exemplified by Piers Plowman, still has a salvific message. The dreamer internalizes this message — a moral one — through his protean meditations on Christ, who rides as the Samaritan, is nailed to the cross, and is the victorious harrower of hell. The transformation comes from grace, which is the power source of a sacramental religion that like medieval Catholicism embraces all sinners in a collective ritual:

> Y ful eftesones aslepe and sodeynliche me mette
> That Peres þe plouhman was peynted al blody
> And cam in with a cros bifore þe comune peple
> And riht lyke in alle lymes to oure lord Iesu.[5]

[3] Judith Anderson, *The Growth of a Personal Voice*, p. 147. My discussion of *Piers Plowman* has been influenced throughout by two definitive works: Anderson's exploration of the poem as "autobiography" wherein the objective "truths" of "philosophy and theology . . . become progressively personalized" (ibid., p. 4) is central to any discussion of the poem. Elizabeth Kirk's *The Dream Thought of* Piers Plowman is similarly concerned with the developing perception of the dreamer and the manner by which thought is externalized and personalized through allegory, symbols, and events in the poem.

[4] Elizabeth Salter, "*Piers Plowman* and the Pilgrimage to Truth," in Robert J. Blanch, ed., *Style and Symbolism in* Piers Plowman, p. 131.

[5] William Langland, Piers Plowman: *An Edition of the C-Text*, ed. Derek Pearsall, p. 342, 21.5-8. All quotations from the poem are taken from this edition. I have specifically chosen to use the C text for my discussion of *Piers Plowman* because I believe that the author's revisions suggest a greater attempt to clarify the dreamer's role

Christ assumes many guises in the dreamer's visual imagination, but he reveals himself progressively from the intangible to the concrete through the metaphors and symbols of the dreamer's spiritual iconography, derived from scripture. The poem initiates the search for Truth with Holy Church's elusive and mystical language of love: "Loue is plonte of pees, most precious of vertues, / For heuene holde hit ne myghte, so heuy hit first semede, / Til hit hadde of erthe yʒoten hitsilue" (1.148–50).[6] The dreamer, however, cannot translate this complex metaphor into the exemplary figure of Christ and is thus unable to comprehend its meaning. Like all other spiritual biographies, *Piers Plowman* depicts the dreamer's development of a spiritual awareness that infuses sacramental meaning into and thus orders the physical world. Beginning in conversion, this process aligns the dreamer's life with the path of redemption. His understanding, previously narrowed by sin to his own history and experience, expands to the forward-looking, inclusive framework of Christian eschatology. Thus, when he awakes from his vision of the Crucifixion and harrowing of hell in passus 20, the dreamer kneels before the cross in full confidence that the penitential ritual he performs is restorative, and he can now anticipate the prophetic events in the apocalyptic passus that follows.

In signaling the process of the dreamer's spiritual growth, or conversion, the poet borrows the triune metaphor of spiritual ascent that Bonaventure's *Itinerarium* popularized, and whose source lies in the theological and devotional works of Augustine and Bernard of Clairvaux.[7] Contemplatives like Walter Hilton adapted this figurative pattern for works of spiritual instruction. Langland, however, is not concerned with unitive or contemplative experiences in *Piers Plowman*;[8] if

---

as a layperson and emphasize the autobiographical nature of the poem. I also agree with the editor that the "C-revision, being the author's latest revision, presumably represents his latest thinking and therefore, *a priori*, what he is entitled to ask to be remembered by" (intro., p. 10).

[6] For a thorough discussion of the patristic imagery in this description see Patricia Kean, "Langland on the Incarnation," *RES* n.s., 16 (1965): 349–63.

[7] See Lawrence Clopper, "Langland's Trinitarian Analogies as a Key to Meaning and Structure," *M&H*, n.s., 9 (1979): 87–110.

[8] This raises an old dispute among readers of the poem. While not all of the arguments can be cited here, the major sources for discussion are to be found in Edward

there were any doubt about this before, the C text's revisions quell the argument once and for all.

The C text illustrates most clearly that the poet's concern was with moral living and thus the purgative stage of the threefold ascent to God. To emphasize this, he buttressed the autobiographical structure of the poem, adding the Apologia (passus 5) and complex alter egos who impede reformation, such as Recklessness and Active. In summarizing his study of the religious allegory in the C text, E. Talbot Donaldson admits that, while there are "elements suggestive of the unitive condition of the soul," the dreamer's journey down the "anagogic path... seems to have stopped short of its goal."[9] He concludes that the poet was not a monk teaching the way of perfection to other contemplatives but an author "endeavouring to point out the path to anyone who was interested in finding it."[10] To point out the path, however, suggests the beginning of a voyage, rather than arriving at a distant destination. Furthermore, although anyone could begin the journey or ascent, the destination in terms of a religious ideal, the unitive experience, was not considered either necessary or possible for Everyman. But contrition was so considered, and there were devotional practices that facilitated it in the confessional process.

Like Margery Kempe, the dreamer of *Piers Plowman* probes the events of his waking life through interior "dramatized meditations" that function as spiritual explorations upon faith and morals.[11] Joseph

---

Vasta, ed., *Interpretations of* Piers Plowman. These include Henry W. Wells, "The Construction of *Piers Plowman*" (1929); Nevill K. Coghill, "The Character of *Piers Plowman*" (1933); T. P. Dunning, "*Piers Plowman*: An Interpretation of the A-Text" (1937); and S. S. Hussey, "Langland, Hilton, and the Three Lives" (1952). All these articles discuss the threefold ascent to Godhead and perceive in one way or another the three estates as external manifestations or degrees of spiritual progress. Since they depend on the A or B text for their evidence, they are less useful than E. Talbot Donaldson's section entitled "Changes Affecting the Interpretation of Religious Allegory" in what remains that major work of interpretation of the C text: Piers Plowman: *The C-Text and Its Poet*, pp. 156–98. By viewing the personifications of Recklessness, Elde, and Active as facets of the dreamer's own personality, Donaldson opened up the poem to a radically new way of reading it (see pp. 171–76).

[9] Donaldson, *Piers Plowman*, p. 196.

[10] Ibid.

[11] Anderson, *The Growth of a Personal Voice*, p. 19. Also see Nolan, *The Gothic Visionary Perspective*, p. 27. Nolan specifically divides the poem into a series of meditations. She believes that "its complexities, together with the fact of the highly

Wittig describes the cumulative process of spiritual enlightenment in the poem as an "inward journey" in the "tradition of monastic moral psychology," viewing the dreamer's objective as a reformation of the *affectus* that is the soul's source of love and virtue. [12] The word "moral," however, brings us immediately to a fourteenth-century penitential tradition, inherently dramatic in its development, and relying on scripture, as do the climatic scenes in *Piers Plowman*. It seems likely that Langland would draw on the common devotional practice of visual meditation, rather than on monastic moral psychology, in creating a spiritual autobiography so preoccupied with the sacrament of penance. [13]

Meditation on Christ's life externalized the perfect conformity of an individual's will to God's will and was the most efficacious manner of understanding the moral truths of scripture. Meditations on Christ crucified brought the sinner to "perfect penance" or a reciprocal love of Christ, enabling him or her to understand fully the meaning of charity. Afterward this experience enabled the penitent to imitate Christ, or joyfully make restitution to other Christians (21.182–93):

> And when this dede was doen, dobest he thouhte
> And ȝaf Peres power and pardoun he graunted
> To alle manere men, mercy and forȝeuenesse;
> ȝaf hym myhte men to assoyle of alle manere synnes
> In couenaunt þat they come and knoleched to pay

---

personalized character of Will as a model for the quest, would suggest that the poem was to serve the private prayer life of the solitary reader." This may be so, but I prefer to think that Langland's poem, while perhaps influenced by meditative narratives like the gospel harmonies, is foremost a literary creation.

[12] Joseph Wittig, "*Piers Plowman* B, Passus IX–XII: Elements in the Design of the Inward Journey," *Traditio* 28 (1972): 228.

[13] Ibid., p. 211. This raises the crucial point whether or not the author was a monk, which seems irrelevant to me in interpreting the C text, for the dreamer clearly is not a monk. While Morton Bloomfield suggests that the poem's pursuit is a "monastic ideal of perfection," revisions in the C text do not comply with this view (Bloomfield, Piers Plowman *as a Fourteenth-Century Apocalypse*, pp. 5, 43). Far more convincing is Robert Worth Frank's discussion of the emphasis on the active life in the poem: "Prayers and Penance are not confined to contemplatives, nor do they distinguish the contemplative life from the active," but rather, "Do Bet and Do Best are elaborations on the single ultimate principle of moral action provided at the conclusion of Do Wel"; see Frank, Piers Plowman *and the Scheme of Salvation*, pp. 30–35. Frank denies that *Piers Plowman* depicts a unitive vision (p. 111).

> To Peres pardoun þe plouhman, *Redde quod debes.*
> Thus hath Peres power, be his pardoun payed,
> To bynde and to vnbynde bothe here and elles
> And assoile men of alle synnes, saue of dette one.
> Anoon aftur an heyh vp into heuene
> He wente, and woneth there, and wol come at þe laste
> And rewarde hym riht wel that *reddet quod debet*, ...

The dreamer cannot assume the responsibility for the spiritual welfare of his fellow Christians unless he first cleanses himself and pays his own debt of love to God. In *Piers Plowman* he cannot do this until he experiences, or beholds, divine love in a recognizable form: "'*Liberum-dei-arbitrium* for loue hath undertake / That this Iesus of his gentrice shal iouste in Pers armes, / In his helm and in his haberion, *humana natura*'" (20.20–22).

When Holy Church appears to the dreamer, she asks: "'Wille, slepestou?'" (1.5). Given the previous tableaux of humankind lulled into a form of idolatry by "'worschip in this world'" (1.8), she might rephrase the question: "Are you also willful and lost in this maze?" Will's request that Holy Church teach him how to save his soul suggests that he is, indeed, lost; yet his recognition of his spiritual plight and realization that he cannot of his own power find salvation signal that he can be reformed. As Dante so painfully illustrated in the *Inferno*, the unredeemable are those who never admit their sins and hence cannot seek forgivness.

The advice Holy Church gives the dreamer, who seeks a "kynde knowyng," or experiential knowledge of Truth, seems rather simple:[14]

---

[14] See Kirk, *The Dream Thought of* Piers Plowman, p. 27; also see Britton J. Harwood, "Langland's Kynde Knowyng and the Quest for Christ," *MP* 80 (1983): 242–55; his *"Piers Plowman*: Fourteen Century Skepticism and the Theology of Suffering," *BuR* 19 (1971): 119–36; Mary Clemente Davlin, "Kynde Knowyng as the Major Theme in *Piers Plowman* B," *RES*, n.s., 22 (1971): 1–19. Harwood's discussion of intuitive cognition in the first article cited is of particular interest, for it develops an interesting parallel with visual meditation in its definition of the *notitia intuitiva*: "'Intuitive' here means nothing instinctive or mysterious; rather, it simply derives from *intueri*, 'to gaze at, pay attention to.'... In evident knowledge of Christ, the concept signified by 'Christ' would be caused by an existing and present object" (p. 245). In addition, Harwood suggests that, "while both Scotus and Ockham agreed that *notitia intuitiva* might be supernaturally provided, 'kynde knowyng' has not come so for Will" (p. 247). Harwood thus raises important questions about the dreamer's epistemology and the role vision or meditation plays in it in the broader context of fourteenth-century philosophy.

"'...to louye thy lord leuest of alle, / Dey rather þen do eny dedly synne'" (1.142–43). She explains that he must love first, and then love will actively manifest itself in virtuous living. Acts of virtue are of little value if they are not grounded in love (1.177–80):

> "But yf ȝe louye leeliche and lene þe pore,
> Of such good as god ȝow sent goodliche parte,
> Ȝe na haueth na more meryte in masse ne in oures
> Then Malkyn of here maydenheed when no man here
>   couayteth."

At the outset of the dreamer's spiritual journey, therefore, Holy Church sets forth her dogma on salvation. All of the sacraments of the Church cannot save one who lacks the love that provides the impetus for an apostolic life. To go through the meaningless motions, as do the friars who absolve sinners who are not contrite is to nourish the sinfulness that disintegrates both individual and society as mercilessly as the plague.[15] Passus 1 establishes the dilemma of the spiritual child before conversion or contrition. The dreamer must learn what love is, but like any child he can only do this through *imitatio*, or the actual experience of being loved. This is "kynde knowyng" (1.161–64):

> "For of kynde knowynge of herte ther comseth a myhte
> And þat falleth to þe fader þat formede vs alle,
> Lokede on vs with loue, let his sone deye
> Mekeliche for oure mysdedes to amende vs alle, ..."

If the dreamer is to understand the nature of love, he can do so only through a direct and recognizable encounter with love, or the Incarnation, which manifested perfect love to humanity.

But the dreamer, like the other folk on the field, is as yet unprepared for this revelation. His reaction to the appearance of Lady Meed discloses his spiritual state in greater detail. Immediately his heart is "raueschede" (2.16) by Meed's rich clothing, a dramatization of the dreamer's own *cupiditas*, which is similar to the varied kinds of idolatry visible in the actions of the folk on the field. The poet chose the word "ravish" for two reasons. First, it has immediate sexual connotations that are appropriate to a venality figure like Meed, whose prostitution,

---

[15] On the nature of sin see Kirk, *The Dream Thought of* Piers Plowman, pp. 49–51.

125

and thus malevolence, results from the desires of those who behold and objectify her.[16] "Ravischen" also had spiritual connotations certainly known to Langland. Wolfgang Riehle notes that in expressing "ecstasy the English [mystical] texts seem to use almost exclusively the verb *ravishen*, which is etymologically related to *rapere* or *raptus*."[17] The word suggests a spiritual submission to an overpowering divine love that is emotionally and physically transforming. The sexual metaphor appears in its most sublime form in the metaphysical poetry of John Donne:

> That I may rise, and stand, o'erthrow mee,' and bend
> Your love, to break, blowe, burn and make me new...
> Except you enthrall mee, never shall be free
> Nor ever chast, except you ravish mee.[18]

What Langland depicts in the dreamer's reaction to Meed is therefore an unnatural inversion of love, or the substitution of a tawdry, insubstantial feeling for a heightened religious experience. Holy Church directed Will to "'louye thy lord leuest of alle'" (1.142), and this he cannot do. Without grace the dreamer cannot properly render his debt of love to God and is wandering dangerously near the deep dale himself.

In the C text Langland added the Apologia to clarify the dimensions of the spiritual journey upon which the dreamer embarks. If the transition from passus 4, with its political drama, to the dreamer's internal voice of passus 5 seems abrupt, we must look for the patterns within the poem that such narrative movement initiates. Except for passus 4, all of the opening passages begin with an insistent "I," locating the reader's perspective. The focus then consistently broadens to the panoramic scenes that evoke questions about the reformation of Christian society in both secular and ecclesiastical realms. In passus 4 the dreamer's voice nearly disappears as he observes the conclusion of the complex allegory examining Meed's role in the kingdom.

[16] See A. G. Mitchell, "Lady Meed and the Art of *Piers Plowman*," in Blanch, ed., *Style and Symbolism in* Piers Plowman, pp. 174–93.

[17] Riehle, *The Middle English Mystics*, p. 94.

[18] John Donne, *The Divine Poems*, ed. Helen Gardner, p. 11, no. 10, lines 3–4, 13–14.

Conscience and Reason restore a spiritual order within the kingdom and the individual. *Piers Plowman*, however, suggests that the restoration of divine order begins with the private despair and sufferings of individuals. The poem thrusts us back into the personal, experiential world of the Apologia, where Will must live this Christian life that Holy Church never quite explains.[19] There is almost a sense of relief to return with the dreamer to a world of specific places, Cornhulle and London, and of texture and recognizable form. Here Christian eschatology is manifested through ritual, the *"placebo"* and *"dirige"* (5.46), while history and law are revealed through scripture.

"Romynge in remembraunce" with the dreamer recalls the part memory plays in the shaping of any spiritual autobiography (5.11). Memory has the power of recalling past events, summoning the power of the *virtus imaginaria* to reenact them visually.[20] The events the dreamer recollects in passus 5 do not conform tightly to a chronological structure, although we do receive a vague picture of his education as a youth, his choice of livelihood and his marriage. Of all these details the most important is that Will persists in living the "'lyf þat me lykede'" (5.11) in spite of the fact that Reason and Conscience find it unworthy. Like Margery Kempe's *Book*, which leaves out many of the most ordinary details of life and neglects "þe tyme & þe ordyr whan thyngs befellyn" (p. 5, line 16), passus 5 in *Piers* is patterned by the discovery of spiritual truths, which is the typical order of conversion narratives. That is why the external facts of the dreamer's life are less worthy of being chronicled than the reflective dialogue with Reason, who, as the "dreamer's own rational self-analysis" remarks upon Will's wandering from the path of salvation.[21] The passus is reflective, full of subtle ironies implying that the narrative voice is conscious of error and is retelling past events in the present tense from an enlightened perspec-

---

[19] Bloomfield writes that in *Piers Plowman* "sharp lines separate one line from another but the background of depth seems missing . . . . the concrete element seems to be at war with itself" (Piers Plowman *as a Fourteenth-Century Apocalypse*, p. 41). This tension is evident in Margery Kempe's *Book* as well and is characteristic of the movement in both texts between spiritual, dreamlike, or meditative experience and the immediate, concrete experience of the physical world.

[20] Gilson, *The Philosophy of St. Bonaventure*, pp. 327–28.

[21] Langland, *Piers Plowman*, ed. Pearsall, p. 98n.

tive. The passus thus shares the autobiographical structure of Kempe's *Book* or Augustine's *Confessions*.

It is particularly revealing that in both the Apologia of *Piers* and the first chapter of Margery's *Book* "Concience" ("conscyens" in the *Book*, p. 6, line 33) plays a key role in bringing the sinner to a sense of wrongdoing. Conscience, as Langland tells us in passus 16 (line 191) is "'goddes clerk and his notarie,'" recalling debts and deciding what acts to "'chalenge or chalenge nat'" (16.190) when reviewing the sinner's life. This moral faculty, accompanied by Reason, is therefore necessary in constructing a spiritual autobiography. In both passus 5 and the preconversion sections of the *Book*, Will and the unredeemed Margery rebel against Conscience's better judgement.

While Conscience urges Margery to confess a secret deed she has long kept to herself, causing her to make faulty confessions, the devil tells her "whyl sche was in good heele hir nedyd no *con*fessyon but don penawns be hir-self a-loone, & all schuld be for3ouyn, for God is me*r*cyful j-now" (p.7, lines 2–5). Although she fasts and prays, exhibiting all the signs of contrition, Margery has not cleansed her heart because "sche wold not schewyn it in confessyn" (p. 7, line 8). What follows is a period of despair typical in conversion stories when, suffering from extremely poor health, Margery faces the prospect of damnation. The *Book* illustrates that spiritual rebellion, or willfulness, is a far greater danger to Margery's salvation than her forgivable, hidden sin.

Langland follows the same conversional pattern in his depiction of Will. While he lives his idle, self-serving life, he reaches a point where Conscience appeals to him, pointing out his errors (5.6–10):

> For as y cam by Consience with Resoun y mette
> In an hot heruest whenne y hadde myn hele
> And lymes to labory with and louede wel fare
> And no dede to do but to drynk and to slepe.
> In hele and in inwitt oen me apposede.

The word "harvest" here is clearly akin in meaning to the spiritual potency dramatized in the Parable of the Vineyard. Christ calls his laborers to worthy vocations, and they are to work unquestioningly. Like Margery, the dreamer errs gravely in thinking that his physical "hele" is a reason to ignore his spiritual "hele." And like Margery, he stubbornly insists on being his own physician, taking half measures in attending to his spiritual welfare (5.36–39):

> "My fader and my frendes foende me to scole,
> Tyl y wyste witterly what holy writ menede
> And what is beste for the body, as the boek telleth,
> And sykerost for þe soule, by so y wol contenue."

He also assumes that external penances without contrition will suffice: "For in my consience y knowe what Crist wolde y wrouhte. / Preyeres of a parfit man and penaunce discret / Is the leuest labour þat oure lord pleseth" (5.83–85). The dreamer falls into the same simplistic and fallacious reasoning that Margery does; when and if his good health fails, he can rely on God's mercy, like the thief on the cross who begs for mercy at the last opportunity.

This attitude must have been fairly prevalent, for it is sternly addressed in *Handlyng Synne* (lines 4789–93):

> And, sum men, yn alle here lyve,
> Clenly ne wyle þey hen shryve;
> For þey synne alle yn hope of grace,
> At here endyng wene þey have space;
> Þan þenke þey to shryve hem clene:
> To suyche men, God shewep hys tene.[22]

Langland further projects the besmirching of Will's soul by Meed through the specifically commercial terms of Will's language. According to Christian dogma, Christ paid the ransom, the "bote," for mankind freely through his death on the cross. Thus sinful humanity has no bargaining power for salvation through good works or any other means but God's love alone. The dreamer has not yet realized this essential truth (5.92–98):

> "That is soth," y saide, "and so y beknowe
> That y haue ytynt tyme and tyme myspened;
> Ac ȝut, I hope, as he þat ofte hath ychaffared
> And ay loste and loste, and at þe laste hym happed
> A bouhte suche a bargayn he was þe bet euere,

---

[22] Robert Manning of Brunne, *Handlyng Synne*, p. 59, lines 4789–93.

> And sette al his los at a leef at the laste ende,
> Suche a wynnyng hym warth thorw wordes of grace."

The dreamer's presumption "that alle tymes of my tyme to profit shal turne" (5.101) indicates that he has little understanding of the Passion and what was accomplished on Calvary for his benefit.

The penitential scene that follows the dreamer's discourse with Reason and Conscience is also reminiscent of Margery's penances. Without contrition, the dreamer's gestures are mechanical and meaningless, for they do not remove the root of sin—wilfullness (5.105–108):

> And to þe kyrke y gan go, god to honoure,
> Byfore þe cross on my knees knokked y my brest,
> Syʒing for my synnes, seggyng my *pater-noster*,
> Wepyng and waylyng til y was aslepe.

Among several confessional scenes in the poem this is the first preparation for penance that the dreamer enacts. As Elizabeth Kirk has noted in reference to the A text (which is applicable here), Will the dreamer now enters the poem as the human will.[23] To this point the only other confession that we have seen is Meed's false performance of the sacrament without contrition in passus 3. This scene dramatically illustrates that without a reformation of the will there is little value in the actions that accompany shrift, such as absolution or prayers performed afterward. In her discussion of attrition and contrition in *Piers Plowman*, Greta Hort explains that "the attrite sinner was in a perilous state, unless it was possible to turn his attrition into contrition."[24] Under the stern advice of Conscience and Reason the dreamer goes to the church to consider his sins, but Langland intentionally focuses on the dreamer's external actions rather than the state of his heart. The inadequate confessions of the Seven Deadly Sins that immediately follow this scene should indeed make the reader wonder whether the poet is quietly telling us about the dreamer's own attrition.[25]

---

[23] Kirk, *The Dream Thought of* Piers Plowman, p. 49.

[24] Hort, *Piers Plowman*, p. 139.

[25] Kirk writes, "Finally, the confessions which follow are not merely those of individual folk on the field but also those of the Dreamer" (*The Dream Thought of* Piers Plowman, p. 49).

All of the sins of which humanity is culpable appear in passus 6 and 7. While the dreamer is certainly not guilty of all of them, they all display a childish egocentrism, a pettiness, that is usually associated with the human condition and its narrow perspective in medieval literature. Reason makes a subtle connection between Will and the rebellious lot when he bids the sinful "wastours" to "worche and wynne here sustinaunce / Thorw som trewe trauail and no tyme spille," as he bade Will earlier in the passus (5.126–27). The confessions of the deadly sins aptly show that sin, which ever remains in a state of sin by its nature, cannot confess properly; hence neither can a sinner who adheres to a sinful life.[26]

The sins do not produce "model confessions," as Greta Hort erroneously concluded,[27] but are outward, empty acts that parody the sacrament. There is an uncomfortable likeness between Will, who is induced "to wepe water with his eyes" (6.2) and Purnelle, who zealously cries to the heavens and wishes to wear a hair shirt. The image evokes the episode from Margery's *Book* when, in an early stage of her conversion, she insists on wearing a hair shirt as a penance. In one of her most eloquent meditations Christ assures her that this is unnecessary (p. 16, lines 32–38; p. 17, lines 1–9):

> I am comyn to þe, Iheſu Cryst, þat deyd on þe Crosse sufferyng byttyr peynes & passyons for þe. I, þe same God, forȝefe þe þi synnes to þe vtterest poynt.... Þerfor I bydde þe & comawnd þe, boldly clepe me Iesus, þi loue, for I am þi loue & schal be þi loue wyth-owtyn ende. And, dowtyr, þu hast an hayr vp-on þi bakke, I wyl þu do it a-way, & I schal ȝiue þe an hayr in þin hert þat schal lyke me mych bettyr þan alle þe hayres in þe world.

Langland draws his portraits of the sins and their false confessions with dark humor: Envy persists in cursing his enemies; Wrath is impatient with his penances; and Covetyse, who is not even attrite and therefore will not make restitution, cannot be absolved of his sin even conditionally. Covetyse is in an especially dangerous predicament, for he knowingly makes a mockery of the external act of penance (6.272–76; italics added):

---

[26] See ibid., p. 50.
[27] Hort, *Piers Plowman*, p. 149.

> "In haly dayes at holy churche when y herde masse
> Ne hadde *y neuere will* witterly to byseche
> Mercy for my mysdedes pat y ne mourned ofter
> For loos of good, leef me, then for lycames gultes.
> As, thow y deddly synne dede, y dradde nat so sore."

As Covetyse himself states, he lacks the will to amend himself and thus receive God's mercy. All of the sins share this essential aspect of Sin, constituting "a collective portrait of the diseased human will" that culminates in Sloth, who is "a paralysis of the will itself; thus, Sloth is distinguised in the C-text by introducing passus 7."[28] Ironically, like the dreamer, who is also idle to a lesser degree and wayward, Sloth opens his confession by dramatically knocking his breast as a sign that he is penitent. However readily he goes through the motions of confession, he forgets just as quickly. He never performs penance, he forgets vows, and "'yf y bidde eny bedes, but yf hit be in wrath, / That y telle with my tonge is ten myle fro myn herte'" (7.16–17). Even worse, "'Goddes payne and his passioun is puyre selde in my thouhte'" (8.20). Consequently Sloth admits that he never performs those acts of charity that characterize the apostolic life of virtue.

As Walter Hilton explained in the *The Ladder of Perfection*, even unenlightened men can practice virtues because reason tells them that this is good or because of "the fear of God."[29] For these works to constitute charity, however, they must be performed in imitation of Christ: "But when, by the grace of Jesus and as a result of spiritual exercises and bodily discipline, acts prompted by reason alone become prompted by enlightenment, and acts of will become acts of charity, then this man has a love of virtue."[30] Sloth cannot be charitable because his will is diseased. His spiritual predicament thus mirrors the dreamer's own. Will cannot make restitution, cannot live fully as a Christian until he discovers that a man's form of living reflects the harmony of his will with God's.[31] This is not necessarily achieved

---

[28] Kirk, *The Dream Thought of* Piers Plowman, p. 59.

[29] Hilton, *The Ladder of Perfection*, p. 14.

[30] Ibid.

[31] See David Mills, "The Role of the Dreamer in *Piers Plowman*," in S. S. Hussey, ed., *Piers Plowman: Critical Approaches*, pp. 180–212. Also see W. O. Evans, "Charity in *Piers Plowman*," in Hussey, ed., *Piers Plowman*, pp. 245–78. Evans notes: "It is

through the contemplative life, because Piers himself exemplifies Christian life as a pilgrim plowing the earth for his fellow Christians' sustenance. The true pilgrim, as Piers emphasizes in passus 8, is one who seeks God in his heart first, rather than the ancient traveler who wears a pilgrim's costume but has no idea where Truth dwells.

The pardon scene clarifies the poet's views on the disparity between external acts and sincere spiritual motivation. Love of Christ begins in grace and moves men and women to Do-well by leading them further into a state of grace. Although pilgrimages, pardons, and prayer belong to Truth's way, they are somewhat like Margery and Purnelle's hair shirt. They are of limited value if the penitent's heart remains hardened because of sin. As the poet clarifies in the C text, "Ac to truste vp this trionales, treuly me thynketh / Hit is nat so syker for þe soule, certes, as ys Dowel" (9.332–33).

The dreamer's waking encounter with the friars in passus 10, rather than being a biting satire on the Minorites, further exposes his misapprehension of "Truth" as a speculative knowledge rather than a manner of living. The firar's "forbisene" offers a simple analysis of humanity's cupidity and emphasizes God's mercy in providing a remedy for sin in the sacraments of the church. The exemplum is dogmatically sound and appropriate here, for it speaks directly to the dreamer of his own spiritual state. The metaphor illustrates that humankind's stability lies not in itself but in God, who created man with a free will. Even when man fails, however, he may remove himself from the danger of sin through contrition, confession, and restitution: "'. . . haue we no reste til we restitue / Oure lyf to oure lord god for our lycames gultes'" (10.54–55). This advice anticipates a major theme in the poem, and through it the friar expeditiously points the dreamer in the right direction for his pursuit of "Truth." The error lies not with the friar but with the dreamer who is too impatient to heed it and thus wanders alone in the "wilde wilderness," a landscape externalizing his spiritual predicament.[32]

---

relevant to our consideration of charity to realize that it not only is the heavenly pattern of hierarchy mirrored in earth, but also that all acts of kindness and courtesy practiced on earth have their source in God and are themselves a mirror, or rather extension, of life in heaven" (p. 267).

[32] Frank remarks that it is "unsatisfactory to dismiss the scene with the friars as irrelevant satire," insisting that the poet treats them "respectfully." See Piers Plowman *and the Scheme of Salvation*, pp. 48–49.

The dreamer now embarks upon his search for an intellectual knowledge of Do-well that proves as frustrating as it is fruitless. Dame Study instructs him to learn to love, but that is not as easy as it sounds. The only "doctour" (11.136) is an exemplary love for which the dreamer seems to seek in all of the wrong places. As Joseph Wittig suggests, the dreamer's error lies in seeking intellectual knowledge instead of focusing on moral reformation through *affectus*.[33] In the process of reformation Will must recognize the importance of revelation as an assurance and a directive.[34] Through the incarnation, God provided all of humanity with the assurance of salvation and an example of how to live. Lacking faith in Providence as a spiritually ordering energy, the dreamer falls prey to the unredeemed life that "fortune" imposes on those who cannot align their lives to the pattern of Christ's. Comforted by the immediate necessities of the world, the physical demands of the flesh and simple desire, the dreamer is once more "rauysched" (11.169) or ensnared in the state of spiritual inversion that is idolatry. What he sees in the "myrrour þat hihte myddelerde" (11.171) is the world through his own disordered perspective for it reflects "an exact image of falsehood."[35] At this point the narrative of *Piers Plowman* clearly exhibits the reflexive or self-reflective mode of spiritual autobiography. The passus does indeed have the stark desperation of Augustine's plea when he was similarly trapped in "þe lond of longyng" (11.170) before fleeing to Carthage: "And I became unto myself thereby a land of want and misery."[36]

Spiritual autobiography is conversional, and without this painful self-evaluation the individual can never wrench himself or herself from the familiar path of sin to the eschatological path of salvation Chris-

[33] Wittig, "*Piers Plowman* B," pp. 221.

[34] On the primacy of revelation over knowledge in *Piers Plowman* see Kirk, *The Dream Thought of* Piers Plowman, p. 119.

[35] See Langland, *Piers Plowman*, ed. Pearsall, p. 202n.; Wittig, "*Piers Plowman* B," p. 239. Particularly germane to any literary exposition of the mirror image in *Piers Plowman* is Ritamary Bradley, "The Speculum Image in Medieval Mystical Writers," in Glasscoe, ed., *The Medieval Mystical Tradition in England*, pp. 9–27. Bradley explains: "With overtones from the medieval theory of sense perception, the eye is passive and receives a faithful image, if it is healthy and clear" (p. 11). She also established the mirror metaphor's use in fourteenth-century spiritual literature aimed at the beginner rather than the contemplative.

[36] Augustine, *Confessions*, p. 47.

tianity presents to all believers. James Olney, however, sees this critical process as belonging to all forms of biography, which ultimately extends from the isolated individual's need to create patterns and thus meaning in life: "With his yearning for order...man explores the universe continually for laws and forms not of his own making..., but what, in the end, he always finds is his own face: a sort of ubiquitous, inescapable man-in-the-moon, which, if he will, he can recognize as his own mirror-image.[37]

The dreamer is essentially back where he was in passus 5 — Concupiscence assures him that she will "sewe" his "wille" (11.184), and he proceeds to live the life that he likes, with little care for approaching age and the worry that he will need to justify his actions at some future point. As before, his Recklessness plies him with the false security that " 'þou hast ful fer to elde' " (11.197). The dreamer persuades himself, as he did before in his debate with Reason, that his salvation depends on God's mercy (11.255–62):

> "A Gode Friday, y fynde, a feloun was ysaued
> That vnlawefulliche hadde ylyued al his lyf-tyme,
> And for he biknewe on þe croes and to Crist shrof hym
> He was sunnere ysaued then seynt Iohn þe Baptiste
> . . . .
> Withoute penaunce oþer passioun oþer eny other peyne. . . .

This passage presents the serious nature of the dreamer's spiritual crisis, for without accepting the Passion as the prerequisite for his own salvation, he is utterly lost. As Elde and Holiness prophesy: " 'That wit shal turne to wrechednesse for Wil hath al his wille!' " (12.2).

Elizabeth Kirk has claimed that "repentence begins, not with spectacular withdrawal from major crimes, but with the unspectacular fundamental acceptance that man is not his own master."[38] The dreamer's healing begins when Kynde displays the world in all its symmetry. The experience of beholding God's will manifested in all of creation teaches the dreamer about perfect order, but, more importantly, points to the Incarnation as the locus of all human experience. Under Reason's tutelage the dreamer Will revises his presumptuous

[37] Olney, *Metaphors of Self*, p. 4.
[38] Kirk, *The Dream Thought of* Piers Plowman, p. 53.

theory that one can be saved without pain. God created a world in which pain reminds humanity of sin; in an eminently reasonable act God allowed his son to experience man's sin to show that man was capable of defying sin: "'Ho soffreth more then god?' quod he; 'no gome, as y leue! / He myhte amende in a mynte-while al þat amys standeth, / Ac he soffreth, in ensaumple þat we sholde soffren alle'" (13.196–98).

Having stepped outside his own chaotic apprehension of the world to experience a divine order imposed on even the most insignificant creatures, the dreamer is now prepared, with the aid of Imaginative, to survey his own experience with the hope of finding a similar order. Judith Anderson has defined Imaginative's function most succinctly: with the aid of memory and reason, he makes "meaningful connections among the Dreamer's earlier positions, viewing them with a different attitude and in a new light."[39] Specifically, Imaginative affirms Clergy's rightful role in teaching penance. Because Clergy recognizes sin and the importance of contrition, Clergy can help those who have rationalized or submerged their sins to make a proper confession (14. 114–22):

> "For yf þe clerke be connynge he knoweth what is synne
> And how contricion withoute confessioun conforteth þe soule,
> And we seen in þe sauter, in psalmes oen or tweyne,
> How contricioun is comended for hit cacheth awey synne:
>
> . . . .
>
> There þe lewede lyth stille and loketh aftur lente
> And hath no contricion ar he come to shrifte, and thenne can he lytel telle,
> But as his loresman hym lereth byleueth and troweth, ..."

Imaginative assures the dreamer once and for all that relying on God's mercy while ignoring his law is imprudent. With the good sense that characterizes his personification, Imaginative explains that the dreamer's hope of being saved like the "'feloun þat a Goed Fryday was saued'" is unreasonable (14.141). In contrast to the thief, those believers who follow God's law, as do the saints, maidens, martyrs, and widows, are secure in heaven and "'Hit were no resoun ne riht to rewarde bothe ylyche'" (14.147). Having chosen rightly and freely, they will have the greater reward.

[39] Anderson, *The Growth of a Personal Voice*, p. 34.

The appearance of Active in passus 15 again confirms the auto-biographical structure of the C text. Whereas in the B-Text this figure emerges as Haukyn, who represents all of humanity, as Active he corresponds more closely to the dreamer's own spiritual predicament. In contrast to the Apologia, where the dreamer has confessed that he is idle and irresponsible in contributing to the practical needs of his community, in this passus Active overcompensates for the dreamer's youthful faults by focusing too much on the world's physical welfare and not enough on his own spiritual health. Neither state is presented as superior to the other, for both fail to pull the dreamer's external life into harmony with his spiritual duties. Neither state realizes his Christian potential for charity, which is the virtue that both reigns in the heart and manifests itself in works. As Patience explains to Active: "'Meeknesse and mylde speche and men of o will, / The whiche wil loue lat to oure lordes place'" is "charite," and humanity can discover true charity only by conforming the sinful will to God's (15.275–76). Holy Church has given humankind a "chartre" (16.36) to help it achieve this end. The charter is the sacrament of penance, which legally exempts all individuals from sin, should they so choose, and directs them to the "trewe welle" (16.40) of love and virtue, which must be the motivation for all their actions. Patience is very meticulous in defining the three stages that constitute a thorough confession—"*Cordis contricio, Oris confessio,* [and] *Operis satisfaccio*" (16.32). Good works naturally follow spiritual reformation, and whether the dreamer plays the vagabond or Active, he must make a full confession, "Elles is al an ydel al oure lyuynge here" (16.38). Patience's review of the Seven Deadly Sins is not redundant in this context, for he presents them from an enlightened perspective (rather than the sinful one necessarily inherent in their own self-projections) and clarifies their obstruction to the apostolic life of patient poverty that the dreamer seeks.

Because Active is one of the dreamer's personae, unlike Haukyn, the poet also omitted the repentance scene of the B text at this point in the poem, and instead we have the dreamer's meeting with Liberum Arbitrium.[40] This makes good sense, for the dreamer is still un-

---

[40] For Donaldson's theories on the revision in the C text see Donaldson, *Piers Plowman*, pp. 175–77.

prepared for the vision of the Crucifixion that transforms him. In defining the nature of charity for the dreamer, Liberum Arbitrium points out that being Christlike cannot be narrowly prescribed by external conditions but is a quality of life that stems from spiritual joy. He asserts that charity can be found in many ways of life, by kings and beggars both, but it is foremost an active vocation of doing God's will.

In passus 1 the dreamer begged Holy Church to tell him how he might save his soul. This is in keeping with his egocentrism, his solitary, preferred life as a marginal cleric without obligation to a regular flock or community. Fourteenth-century spirituality and the movements it fostered, like the *devotio moderna*, urgently stressed the outward-looking nature of Christianity, as does Langland. The business of Christians is to live like Christ serving others. Therefore, when at the beginning of passus 18 the dreamer asks Liberum Arbitrium to "'teche me to Charite'" (18.1) he begins his journey anew in the right spirit — looking outward. It is a paradox of Christian theological tradition that penitents must first search for the image of God in their own souls before *imitatio* is possible.

Like Bonaventure in the *Lignum vitae*, Langland creates an allegorical tree to illustrate God's potency in the individual soul as well as in history.[41] This section of the poem is richly evocative, and a simple analysis of its various meanings would be insufficient and inappropriate here. On one level, however, as with Bonaventure's tree, the function of this image is meditative. It does not offer an explanation of divine order but encapsulates it and presents it to the dreamer's sight that he may imprint it on his memory, or internalize it as a frame of reference for the events to come. Thus, as in Bonaventure's text, it provides an eschatological structure for the impending meditations on Christ's life. In considering this most complex image in *Piers Plowman* in the context of an English mystical tradition, A. V. C. Schmidt concludes that, unlike illuminative visions, such those of Julian of Norwich, Langland is not concerned with creating an image that offers an

---

[41] While my study cannot discuss the allegory of the Tree of Charity, a survey of various readings in this section of the poem can be found in David Aers, Piers Plowman *and the Christian Allegory*, pp. 79–84, followed by a discussion of his own ideas. Also see Anderson, *The Growth of a Personal Voice*, pp. 135–41; and Kirk, *The Dream Thought of* Piers Plowman, pp. 168–78.

"intellectual explanation" for divine mysteries; for humankind "illumination of God's purpose comes from meditation on the passion."[42] Instead, "The 'menyng' of the tree is the Trinity, not as transcendent Godhead but as the divinity dwelling in man through the grace of Christ's incarnation and death."[43] The image in the Cor-hominis (18.4) therefore emphasizes the nature that man and God shared rather than the other manifestations of the Trinity that are unknowable to the dreamer.

In their narrative movements the sequences that follow this strangely protean image in the "inner dream" have the highly associative quality characteristic of Margery Kempe's meditations. While the scriptural stories of Dives and Abraham and the Good Samaritan form the subject of the meditations, the space in which they move, the passing of time, and their causal connections assume the interior or shadowy dimensions of imaginative vision. As in all other dramatic or participatory meditation, the dreamer's interpretations of these stories reflect their pertinence to his own spiritual dilemma. They are imaginatively re-created as a way of explaining the spiritual truths he wishes to confirm or explore. Hence the dreamer has a likeness in Abraham, who also has yet to experience the salvific joy of the Incarnation and Crucifixion. This episode makes him conscious of the firm hand with which sin held humanity until God through his mercy provided a ransom. This realization marks a measure of progress in the dreamer's spiritual growth, for when he fully understands the human predicament without Christ's intervention on his behalf, he weeps. This is a signal of a changing heart in the dreamer from which the reader can infer that Will is prepared for further revelation, now that he is willing to accept the authority of scripture.

This authority is embodied in the Samaritan, who exemplifies Christian virtue and hence *imitatio* to its most literal degree. Donaldson writes that these passus of the poem persistently objectify virtues, stressing the moral purpose of all scriptural narrative. Consequently, with charity, as with the virtues of humility and patience, "the poet of

---

[42] A.V. C. Schmidt, "Langland and the Mystical Tradition," in Glasscoe, ed., *The Medieval Mystical Tradition in England*, pp. 28, 30.

[43] Ibid., p. 28.

the C [text] emphasizes its external aspects more than the theologian does."[44] Since he is the personification of the apostolic life, the Samaritan appropriately teaches the dreamer that love of one's "emcristene" is the path to salvation. But first one must repent any previous lack of charity with true contrition of heart.

The Samaritan's speech suggests that this is not easy. Sin hardens the heart and leads to a kind of false confidence that the dreamer certainly exhibited in earlier passus (19.286–89):

> "Thus hit fareth bi such folk þat folewen here owene will,
> That euele lyuen and leten nat til lif hem forsake;
> Som drede of disperacion thenne dryueth awey grace
> That mercy in here mynde may nat thenne falle."

God's mercy depends on a complete conversion, or turning from sin: "Ac ar his rihtwisnesse to reuthe turne, restitucion hit maketh, / As sorwe of herte is satifaccioun for suche þat may not paye" (19.294–95). The dreamer has nothing to offer for his own salvation, being totally dependent upon God's mercy. It is therefore only right that he return "sorwe of herte" as a recompense for his willfulness.

In the fourteenth-century tradition of affective devotion, this compunction of heart could be aroused only by a vision of the Crucifixion. Richard Kieckhefer writes in his discussion of fourteenth-century hagiography and devotion to the Passion:

> If patient submission to God's will was an essential foundation for fourteenth-century piety, devotion to the passion went one important step further. Taking Christ's submission to his Father's will as the archetypal manifestation of patience, the saints and their devotees found in it the key to an understanding of God's will. . . . In their devotion to the passion, the saints bowed to the recognition that what God demands in particular is suffering.[45]

Reason rebuked the dreamer in passus 13: "'Ho soffreth more then god?. . .he soffreth, in ensaumple þat we sholde soffren alle'" (lines 196–99). Through visual meditation on the Passion, whether in the gospel harmonies or in lyrics, the individual could vicariously participate in this suffering and thus "imitate" in some small measure Christ's

---

[44] Donaldson, *Piers Plowman*, p. 196.
[45] Kieckhefer, *Unquiet Souls*, p. 89.

own patient submission to God's will. The experience was both purgative and transforming.

Passus 20 opens with references to the purgative Lenten season; in fact, the dreamer's description of himself as one "wolleward and watschoed" (line 1) implies at a first glance that he has finally aligned his own life with the liturgical cycle that imposed a sacramental and commemorative order on the year. In all the previous passus where Will describes his garments, always having falsely adapted external habits as a sign of spiritual life, he is still unreformed. By his own admission he remains "a recheles renk þat recheth nat of sorwe" (20.2). The Samaritan warned him that this attitude leads to despair, and this is indeed suggested in the dreamer's description of his world-weariness.

In discussing the way *Piers Plowman* turns from allegory to drama in scriptural scenes in the latter part of the poem, Kirk perceptively notes that "we see an artist taking modes of thought characteristic of medieval biblical exegesis, and, instead of merely regarding them as a treasury of accepted images and symbols, creating a genuine artistic equivalent for them in his poem, thus giving it a new kind of structure."[46] This is exactly what Franciscan exegesis did through the creation of dramatic scriptural narratives that impressed upon audiences the theological connection between the Crucifixion and the need for individual penance in the vast structure of salvation history. The Crucifixion and harrowing scenes in *Piers Plowman* function on the similar mimetic or incarnational principle as do the narratives of the *Meditations on the Life of Christ* or the *Meditations on the Supper of Our Lord*. The dreamer must envision, and hence experience or participate in, these scenes to attain the grace necessary for his conversion. Most important of all, he must feel the shame and sorrow of the Crucifixion for which he is personally responsible on account of his sin. This sentiment is powerfully dramatized in the scene of Longinus before his conversion (20.91–95):

> "Aȝeyn my will hit was," quod he, "þat y ȝow wounde made!"
> And syhed and saide, "Sore hit me forthenketh;
> Of þe dede þat y haue do y do me in ȝoure grace.

---

[46] Kirk, *The Dream Thought of* Piers Plowman, p. 181.

141

Bothe my lond and my licame at ʒoure likynge taketh hit,
And haue mercy on me, riʒtfol Iesu!" And riht with þat a wepte.

Like the gospel harmonies, or the mystery cycles that they inspired, Langland re-creates the scene in his own world. The purpose of affective meditation on the passion was to make the scene powerfully immediate and utterly real to the penitent. The passion could be relived at any moment as a result, and thus freed in a sense from its liturgical and commemorative position in the Holy Week. Langland intentionally harmonizes the dreamer's private spiritual drama with the great liturgical drama to stress how conversion imbues ritual celebration with new meaning. Nonetheless, his object was to develop, as did Margery Kempe, an intense awareness of Christ crucified to achieve a more profound *imitatio*. The author of the *Meditations on the Life of Christ* writes to the Poor Clare:

> You have seen how many things you had on this day of Pasch; for all these appearances took place in the Paschal day. But perhaps you have heard but have not felt, for perhaps you did not have compassion at the Passion. I believe that if you felt compassion with your whole mind at the Passion . . . you would feel Pasch everywhere. And this may happen on any Sunday, if with all your mind you prepare yourself on Friday and Saturday with the Passion of the Lord.[47]

Certainly this is suggested in *Piers Plowman* when the dreamer is drawn immediately into the Sunday celebration of the Eucharist, performed not only on Easter Sunday but every Sunday.

Like *Pearl*, which is also very delicate and stylized in its treatment of the Crucifixion, *Piers Plowman* does not indulge in a graphic focus on the suffering of Christ. Nonetheless, Langland's description of the Crucifixion is sketched with the profound theological economy that also characterizes the sparse Crucifixion lyrics, that are often (erroneously) thought to be simple in their composition. In two lines he introduces the paradox of the Incarnation, and the marvelous recon-

---

[47] *Meditations on the Life of Christ*, trans. and ed. Ragusa and Green, p. 369. The Latin reads: "Vidisti quoties hodie habuisti Pascha: nam omnes istae apparitiones in die Paschatis fuerunt. Sed forte audisti, sed non sensisti, qui nec forte in passione compassionem habuisti. Credo enim, quod si passione compati scires, et mentem haberes unitam . . . in qualibet vice sentires Pascha. Et hoc de quolibet die dominico contigere posset, si mente integra diebus Veneris et Sabbati, te cum passione Domini praeparares." *Meditationes*, ed. Peltier, chap. 93, p. 621.

ciliation of opposite natures that is the locus of Franciscan theology: "Pitousliche and pale, as prisoun þat deyeth / The lord of lyf and of liht tho leyde his eyes togederes" (20.59–60). Having beheld the defeat of sin in the events that follow this scene, Will gains a "kynde knowynge" of his own salvation. Joyous and enlightened, the dreamer's first impulse confirms his spiritual health. He wakens his wife and daughter from spiritual sleep and bids them to accompany him to mass, after which he will finally be "hoseled" (21.3). This action anticipates his entrance into "Unity," or the Church. Now, rather than living an idle, self-serving life, Will is willing to assume some responsibility for the spiritual welfare of his fellow Christians. The poem cannot end with Will's private conversion, but "in order for Will to choose *bonum in communis*, he must be able to recognize that good."[48]

At the end of the poem Will's joy is marred by anxiety as he surveys the insurmountable task of reforming the sinful world whose offenses have grown more grievous than ever. Readers have misinterpreted the pervasive note of sorrow and destruction at the poem's finale as a sign of the dreamer's "failure to find truth" paralleling "his failure at Christian renewal."[49] Braswell, for example, assumes that "because he never makes a proper confession and subsequent restitution, Will's character cannot develop."[50] That is not so. If Will were the hermit he first claims to be or a contemplative, perhaps he might have had a unitive vision that would have enabled him to transcend the field of folk with all its weighty cares. But Will is neither. I hope to have demonstrated that he does indeed experience contrition in the poem and may now begin the process of restitution in a rather unremarkable manner in keeping with the life of the ordinary Christian. Because *Piers Plowman* is largely penitential in nature, Will is always drawn back to moral concerns in the realm where Christians are to practice virtue heroically in face of sin and death. Conversion means a turning from sin as a way of life, rather than the life completely free of sin. In his spiritual autobiography, Augustine explains that learning to live righteously on earth is only a beginning:

---

48 Braswell, *The Medieval Sinner*, p. 80.
49 Ibid.
50 Ibid.

> And we at one time were inclined to do well, when our heart had conceived of Thy Holy Spirit; whereas formerly, forsaking thee, we were moved to do ill; but Thou, O God, the One and the Good, didst never cease to do good. And some good works there are of ours, by Thy gifts, but not eternal; after them we hope to rest in Thy great hallowing. But Thou, the Supreme Good that needest no good, art ever at rest, because thou thyself art that rest.[51]

From the friar in passus 10 Will ascertained that spiritual rest begins with restitution. The task remaining for him, therefore, is to complete the penitential triad by performing this restitution. Throughout *Piers Plowman*, Langland insists that purgation leads to an active manifestation of Christ's charity in the world. To Do-Best is thus to assert God's love in society through the *spiritus paraclitus* (21.206), thereby strengthening the Church against disorder and evil, personified by Antichrist. In accordance with the Pauline text (1 Cor. 12:4), Will must reconsider his vocation from an enlightened perspective. Grace's description of the many vocations acceptable to God imposes a new order on the field of folk, all of whom are now called, like Piers himself, as evangelists.

That Unity's cornerstone rests on Christ's Passion (21.322–29) further emphasizes the church's willingness to shelter all who have properly repented. Passus 21 focuses on the difficulty of making restitution, posing a critical problem for penitents like the "breware," who expect penance to be a simple admission of sin and forgivness. The penultimate passus in the poem grimly maintains that self-interest halts the spiritual progress of all but the most committed Christians. The note of anxiety controlling the final vision stems not only from the picture of collective sin demanding God's retribution but also from the dreamer's sense of helplessness concerning his own restitution. "Heuy-chered" and "elyng in herte" (22.2), Will considers how he must live to manifest the spiritual change that he has undergone. Now aged, depressed, and desperately needy, he turns to Kynde for guidance, whose instruction is familiar: "'Lerne to love'" (22.208). If he can wholly submit himself to love's service, he may pass "throw Contricion and Confessioun" (22.213) and abide in Unity.

Langland returns to the corruption of the friars at this point because

---

[51] Augustine, *Confessions*, p. 448.

they exemplify the failure of the most idealistic order to achieve *imitatio*, or to reconcile the life of the spirit with an appropriate vocation. Further, their fall from their calling "for loue to be holy" (22.252) has corrupted the entire church through their denigration of the role they were given as teachers and confessors of the laity. By neglecting their flock, allowing them to confess without contrition and be shriven without promising restitution, the friars imperil the souls of the ignorant. The issue is particularly germane to the dreamer: having painfully worked through the stages of confession, he prepares himself to enter Unity, only to find it corrupted by immoral clergy and the avaricious friars. Will, like other searching Christians, may have to journey the rest of the way to "truth" independently, as a "pilgrime" guided by Conscience alone (22.380).

While the final passus of *Piers Plowman* fail to provide specific answers to the personal and collective spiritual dilemmas the poem defines, they are not entirely negative. As the dreamer's visions become more chaotic, he is more insistent on writing them down upon awakening. This "fiction" reminds the reader that the poem is itself a positive search for order imposed on experiences that ultimately confirm a divine plan already revealed to the dreamer (and the poet) through scripture. In trying to make sense of these enmeshed dreams and memories, the poet and dreamer merge to assert the primacy of the human imagination, which, by mirroring God's greater act of ordering, participates in it.

6

Conclusion

In his *Introduction to the Franciscan Literature of the Middle Ages*, John Fleming concluded that the critera adopted by literary historians to define works as "Franciscan" must necessarily extend beyond authorship to the larger dimension of style, treatment, and subject matter.[1] Nicholas Bozon, William Herebert, and John Grimstone were only a few of the hundreds of English friars writing, copying, and compiling lyrics, sermons, and gospel harmonies incorporating Franciscan themes in the fourteenth century. In this book I have tried to show that these texts, in conjunction with a rich oral tradition of instruction using scriptural narrative, engendered another genre of literature examining the spiritual growth and experience of the individual. The genre is new not because the experiences themselves assume radically different narrative structures but because they borrow from existing structures usually found in contemplative works and revise them for a broader lay audience.

The Franciscan influence is critical in the development of lay spiritual autobiography, exemplified in England in the late Middle Ages

---

[1] Fleming, *An Introduction to the Franciscan Literature of the Middle Ages*, p. 2.

by *The Book of Margery Kempe*, *Pearl*, and *Piers Plowman*. Whether or not the authors were mystics or contemplatives or lay penitents is immaterial. Each struggled to find a convincing voice describing a vision leading to purgation and conversion, hence re-creating a meditative experience. Franciscan meditation provided penitents with the appropriate subject matter for devotional experiences. Through the embellishment of scriptural texts penitents could directly participate in the truth of the Gospels while exploring the mysteries of human faith and the miracle of God's manifestation in temporal time and space. Franciscan meditation must be viewed as a creative act, evoking imaginative responses that eventually manifested themselves in literary forms, just as the Ignatian meditative exercises of the sixteenth century fostered or contributed to the development of the metaphysical religious poetry in England.[2] In fact, Salter insists that "the debt of St. Ignatius of Loyola, in his sixteenth-century *Spiritual Exercises*, to these earlier exponents of the meditation as an exercise of devotion should be stressed."[3]

One reason this meditative tradition, and its relationship to English literature, may have been overlooked for so long is the negative view of the Franciscans held by earlier critics who mistakenly believed the Franciscan religious psychology to be naïve and as a consequence underestimated the intelligence of the medieval laity. John Fleming and David Jeffrey have addressed this question in their works, as have feminist scholars like Clarissa Atkinson, who has discussed the Franciscan evangelical program's deep understanding of human spirituality and the inclusion of this knowledge in its devotional program as a creative principle.[4] The Franciscans asked for and were duly given papal permission to assume the powerful task of guiding the laity through the passages of life, marked by the sacraments of the church. As humorous or reprobate as are the scathing images of the friars in *Piers Plowman* and *The Canterbury Tales*, both authors naturally identify the Franciscans with sexuality and childbearing, sickness,

<hr/>

[2] Louis Martz, *The Poetry of Meditation*.

[3] Salter, *Nicholas Love's* Myrrour, pp. 178–79.

[4] See Moorman, *A History of the Franciscan Order*, pp. 390–406; also see Fleming, *An Introduction to the Franciscan Literature of the Middle Ages*, pp. 110–89; and Jeffrey, *The Early English Lyric*, pp. 169–230.

death, and penance—all of which momentous human events the church carefully incorporated into the spiritual *itinerarium* of the medieval layperson. Carolly Erikson has rightly criticized the narrow perspective of medieval historians who simply comment on the corruption of the order and then neglect the evidence provided by medieval wills, pointing to the respected position Franciscans held among the laity.[5] She notes:

> To the majority of their supporters, the Franciscans appeared to be quite simply the most visible, most accessible dispensers of the Christian sacraments. A substantial part of their [the laypersons'] religious experience was linked to the Minorite Order: many, if not most of the sermons they heard were Franciscan sermons; the saints they petitioned were often Franciscan saints or *beati*; their confessors too were likely to be Minorites, and the graves that would hold them were often in Franciscan cemeteries.[6]

Indirectly Erikson has hit upon what I believe is the most attractive element the Franciscans offered to the laity through their particular kind of spirituality. In mentioning the Franciscan *beati*, or "blessed," and distinguishing them from the saints, Erikson raises a vital question about the nature of human sanctity in Franciscanism that is central to any discussion of spiritual autobiography of the fourteenth and fifteenth centuries. While every order held forth examples of human perfection to be imitated by all Christians, the Franciscans brought to England a literary tradition that abounds with figures who are outside the strict canonical definition of sainthood and are thus highly accessible examples of a spirituality realized in the world.

Francis's own *Vita* in Bonaventure's *Legenda* served as the order's primary model of one who literally and schematically fashioned his life after Christ's. According to the General Chapter of Paris (1266), every Franciscan convent was to have at least one copy of the *Legenda*.[7] One imagines how frequently this text was read aloud in the refectory, memorized by the friars, and transmitted orally through narrative variations, as well as through fairly faithful translations like that in the *Early South English Legendary*. Bonaventure's *Legenda* affirmed for all

[5] Carolly Erikson, "The Fourteenth-Century Franciscans and Their Critics: Part I," *FS* 35 (1975): 207–35; "Part II," *FS* 36 (1976): 108–47.

[6] Ibid., "Part II," p. 145.

[7] Fleming, *An Introduction to the Franciscan Literature of the Middle Ages*, p. 45.

believers the certain knowledge that miracles occur, that human suffering is repaid with eternal joy, and that *imitatio* is possible if one willingly chooses heavenly over earthly riches. Nonetheless, the conventions of hagiography celebrate the unique nature of those chosen by God for special missions, set apart from ordinary beings who chose Christ and thereby separated and elevated to sainthood. Saints' lives appeal to Christians who properly see their roles in collective terms; their happiness lies in the fact that they have sanctioned but familiar intercessors, perhaps from the same town or province, to pray to for personal guidance and comfort.

To supplement their hagiography, in keeping with their more inclusive spiritual message, the Franciscans compiled other stories that celebrate the minor triumphs of historical personages who were not saints. Fleming has described the *Fioretti* as a text "captured in the midst of an exciting change from literary hagiography to unapolegetic exemplary fiction" whose "materials are those of the former [and whose] narrative conceptions [are] those of the latter."[8] The *Fioretti* is a series of short tales translated into Tuscan from the Latin version of Brother Hugolino of Monte Giorgio's *Actus beati Francisci et sociorum ejus* (1328). Besides their charm, the tales are fascinating because they infuse their local setting with the sacramental and incarnational elements that characterize Francis's own life in the *Legenda*. In the *Fioretti* all of Francis's followers are granted visions and heightened spiritual experiences. In the *Fioretti* the paramystical events that make Francis special become regular and often communal experiences, to be shared as a means of bonding the order. Both the Spiritualist friars in the Marches of Ancona and their sisters come dramatically into contact with the divine in various manifestations. For this reason Fleming describes the *Fioretti* as a "running Pentecost."[9] The stories insistently reestablish the links God forged with humanity through the Holy Spirit at the birth of His new church, fictionally revising the apostolic ideal of the Gospels for Everyman in a contemporary setting. The *Fioretti* depict Francis's followers much like the apostles; although often simple, uneducated men and women, they are equal to the task

---

[8] Ibid., p. 61.
[9] Ibid., p. 62.

of reformation because they ask for and receive grace. Although they are plagued now and then by spiritual doubts and anxieties, their insecurities are eased through visions.

When we carefully examine some of the visionary experiences in the *Fioretti*, however, it becomes clear that they are meditative, or self-created, much like those in the religious dream poetry of the fourteenth century, or in Margery's autobiography. Chapter 44, for example, illustrates how meditations on Christ's Passion enable penitents to enter a spiritual realm where they may explore private fears and emerge, their faith and will strengthened, with a clearer sense of how to conform to Christ. The chapter concerns not Francis, but two friars named Peter and Conrad, who are introduced as *beati*.

One day, while meditating on the Passion, Peter beholds the Virgin Mary, John the Evangelist, and Francis standing at the foot of the cross.[10] The scene is similar to the thirteenth- and fourteenth-century *laudes* and Passion lyrics that open with a visual composition. Clearly Peter has conjured up the scene in his imagination. Yet it is interesting to note that with the addition of Francis at the foot of the cross the scene has been transformed from a traditionally scriptural to a highly personal tableau, much like the tableaux of Margery Kempe's meditations. Francis's sanctity will be the subject of meditation and, indirectly, Peter's spirituality, for Peter has chosen to imitate Christ as a radical Spiritualist in spite of the persecution that the papacy and the Conventualists directed against those who insisted on interpreting literally Francis's rule of poverty. The meditation is a deeply personal externalization of Peter's anxiety over the role of suffering (exemplified by the Passion) and the rewards it holds for those who accept tribulation as God's will. The narrator tells us, in fact, that just before Peter visualized this scene he had been wondering which of the three figures suffered the most from Christ's Passion; the episode is thus a lesson on faith and suffering for the reader.

Naturally the humble friar is terrified to see the three august personages before him so vividly. Saint John comforts him, however, and

[10] Marion A. Habig, ed., *The Little Flowers of St. Francis [Fioretti]*, in *St. Francis of Assisi: Writings and Early Biographies: English Omnibus of the Sources for the Life of St. Francis*, pp. 1402–1403.

151

reassures him that "we are come to console thee in thy doubt."[11] He tells Peter that the Virgin suffered the most with Christ, as befits a mother and the one closest to Christ in her sinless nature. Peter then notices that Francis is wearing a fairer garment than John's; this emblematic detail leads the reader further into the question the meditation explores. Saint John assures Peter that Francis's own garment is fairer because the Minorite "bore viler garments" in the world.[12] Saint John then hands Peter a beautiful robe, symbolically embracing him as one of the elect who have adhered to Christ's strict poverty and thus will merit heavenly rewards. When Saint John attempts to clothe Peter in the robe, however, Peter falls into a daze and cries out for his friend Conrad. The vision immediately vanishes.[13]

The limits of the experience are clearly defined by Peter's inability to accept the robe—a privilege granted only after death. While he lives, he must continue to suffer, like Francis. He cannot enter fully into this spiritual mystery, any more than the *Pearl* dreamer can enter the New Jerusalem. Nonetheless, the vision is a gift of grace reassuring Peter of his vocation; like Margery's meditations, or the dreams in *Piers Plowman*, it occurs at a moment of spiritual crisis necessarily involving questions about the penitent's will. Peter is not a saint but an ordinary human being who has chosen to be holy, who is tempted and troubled, and who finds comfort in the devotional exercises the Francisans popularized to help resolve the fears and doubts of all Christians.

In addition, the imaginative act of meditation that creates a dramatic scene transforms itself in the *Fioretti* into another literary act, the written legend. The legend is both biographical and meditative, for the spiritual elements shape our perception of Peter's life, making this one episode of his existence central and relative to all Christians who seek God's path. His life becomes pertinent to the reader's because he, like the solitary figures in *The Book of Margery Kempe*, *Pearl*, and *Piers Plowman*, must discover the pattern that meshes his private, internal spiritual life with his presence in the world. In achieving this integration in his own day and time, he becomes an exemplary figure. Viewed

[11] Ibid., p. 1402.
[12] Ibid., p. 1403.
[13] Ibid.

in the context of earlier "Franciscan literature," these English works suggest that a stronger bond existed between Continental devotional and literary traditions and English spirituality than hitherto assumed.

In this book I have attempted to construct preliminary historical and literary ties between a widespread Franciscan devotional tradition, visual participatory meditation, and a literary tradition of lay spiritual autobiography in England with which it coincided. That the two phenomena are interdependent seems beyond conjecture. The three English works I have discussed have often been perceived by readers as odd, singular texts, viewed outside a popular devotional context and consequently open to misinterpretation. While each of the works is compelling, a self-conscious work of literature in its own right, each presupposed a certain knowledge or acceptance of spiritual patterns that I hope to have highlighted in this book.

Bibliography

Primary Sources

Augustine. *The Confessions*. Trans. Sir Tobie Matthew. London: Burnes and Oates, 1954.

Bonaventure. *Itinerarium mentis in Deum* [*The Soul's Journey into God*]. 10 vols. In *Opera omnia S. Bonaventurae*. Quaracchi, 1898, 5:293–316.

———. *Legenda S. Francisci* [*Legenda maior, Life of Francis*]. In *Opera omnia S. Bonaventurae*. 10 vols. Quaracchi, 1898, 8:504–64.

———. *The Life of Francis*. In Bonaventure. *Works*. Trans. and ed. Ewert Cousins. New York: Paulist Press, 1978.

———. *Lignum vitae* [*Tree of Life*]. In *Opera omnia S. Bonaventurae*. 10 vols. Quaracchi, 1898, 8:68–87.

———. *Opera omnia S. Bonaventurae*. 10 vols. Quaracchi, 1898.

———. *The Soul's Journey into God*. In Bonaventure. *Works*. Trans. and ed. Ewert Cousins. New York: Paulist Press, 1978.

———. *The Tree of Life*. In Bonaventure. *Works*. Trans. and ed. Ewert Cousins. New York: Paulist Press, 1978.

———. *Works*. Trans. and ed. Ewert Cousins. New York: Paulist Press, 1978.

Chaucer, Geoffrey. *The Works of Geoffrey Chaucer*. 2d ed. Ed. F. N. Robinson. Boston: Houghton Mifflin, 1957.

The Cloud of Unknowing. Ed. Phyllis Hodgson. EETS, o.s., vol. 218. London, 1944. Reprint, 1958.

Davies, R. T., ed. *Medieval English Lyrics*. Evanston, Ill.: Northwestern University Press, 1964.

Donne, John. *The Divine Poems*. Ed. Helen Gardner. Oxford: Clarendon Press, 1959.

Habig, Marion A., ed. *St. Francis of Assisi: Writings and Early Biographies: English*

Omnibus of the Sources for the Life of St. Francis. Chicago: Franciscan Herald Press, 1973.

Hilton, Walter. *The Ladder of Perfection.* Trans. and ed. Leo Shirley-Price. London: Penguin, 1957.

Horstmann, Carl, ed. *The Early South English Legendary.* EETS, o.s., vol. 87, 1887.

Kempe, Margery. *The Book of Margery Kempe.* Ed. Sanford Brown Meech, with notes and appendices by Hope Emily Allen. EETS, o.s., vol. 212. London, 1940. Reprint, 1961.

Langland, William. Piers Plowman: *An Edition of the C-Text.* Ed. Derek Pearsall. Berkeley: University of California Press, 1979.

Manning of Brunne, Robert [Robert Mannyng, or Robert of Brunne]. *Handlyng Synne.* Ed. Frederick J. Furnivall. EETS, o.s., vol. 119, London, 1901.

Meditationes vitae Christi. In *Opera omnia Bonaventurae.* Ed. A.C. Peltier. Paris: Ludovicus Vives, 1868. Vol. 12, pp. 509–630. [Often called *Pseudo-Bonaventure.*]

Meditations on the Life of Christ. Trans. and ed. Isa Ragusa and Rosalie Green. Princeton, N.J.: Princeton University Press, 1961. Reprint, 1977.

Meditations on the Supper of Our Lord. Ed. J. Meadows Cowper. London: EETS, o.s., vol. 60. London, 1985.

Morris, Richard, ed. *Early English Alliterative Poems in the West Midland Dialect of the Fourteenth Century.* London: Oxford University Press, 1864.

Pearl. Ed. E. V. Gordon. London: Oxford University Press, 1953.

The Pearl: *A Middle English Poem.* Ed. Charles Osgood. Boston: D. C. Heath, 1906.

Pearl: *An English Poem of the Fourteenth Century.* 2d ed. Ed. and trans. Sir Israel Gollancz. 1891. Reprint, London: N.p., 1897.

A Talkyng of the Love of God. Ed. M. Salvina Westra. The Hague: M. Nijhoff, 1950.

Secondary Sources

Aers, David. Piers Plowman *and Christian Allegory.* London: Edward Arnold, 1975.

Anderson, Judith H. *Biographical Truth.* New Haven, Conn.: Yale University Press, 1984.

———. *The Growth of a Personal Voice.* New Haven, Conn.: Yale University Press, 1976.

Atkinson, Clarissa. *Mystic and Pilgrim: The Book and the World of Margery Kempe.* Ithaca, N.Y.: Cornell University Press, 1983.

Auerbach, Erich. *Mimesis.* Trans. Willard Trask. Princeton, N.J.: Princeton University Press, 1953.

Bevington, David. *Medieval Drama.* Boston: Houghton Mifflin, 1975.

Bishop, Ian. Pearl *in Its Setting.* New York: Barnes & Noble, 1968.

Blanch, Robert J., ed. *Style and Symbolism in* Piers Plowman. Knoxville: University of Tennessee Press, 1969.

Blenkner, Louis. "The Theological Structure of *Pearl.*" *Traditio* 24 (1968): 43–75. Reprinted in John Conley, ed. *The Middle English* Pearl: *Critical Essays.* Notre Dame, Ind: University of Notre Dame Press, 1979, pp. 220–71.

Bloomfield, Morton. Piers Plowman *as a Fourteenth-Century Apocalypse.* New Brunswick, N.J.: Rutgers University Press, 1961.

Bogdanos, Theodore. *Pearl: Image of the Ineffable*. University Park: Pennsylvania State University Press, 1983.

Bolton, Brenda M. "Mulieres sanctae." In *Sanctity and Secularity: The Church and the World*. Vol. 10 of *Studies in Church History*. Oxford: Basil Blackwell, 1973. Reprinted in Susan Mosher Stuard, ed. *Women in Medieval Society*. Philadelphia: University of Pennsylvania Press, 1976, pp. 141–58.

Borroff, Marie. *"Pearl's* 'Maynful Mone': Crux, Simile, and Structure." In Mary J. Carruthers and Elizabeth D. Kirk, eds. *Acts of Interpretation: the Text in Its Contexts, 700–1600: Essays on Medieval and Renaissance Literature in Honor of E. Talbot Donaldson*. Norman, Okla.: Pilgrim Books, 1982, pp. 159–72.

Bradley, Ritamary. "The Speculum Image in Medieval Mystical Writers." In Marion Glasscoe, ed. *The Medieval Mystical Tradition in England*. Papers Read at Dartington Hall, July, 1984. Cambridge: D. S. Brewer, 1984, pp. 9–27.

Brady, Ignatius. "The History of Mental Prayer in the Order of Friars Minor." *FS* 11 (1951): 317–45.

Braswell, Mary Flowers. *The Medieval Sinner*. Rutherford, N.J.: Farleigh Dickinson University Press, 1983.

Brewer, Derek. *English Gothic Literature*. New York: Schocken Books, 1983.

Brooke, Rosalinde B., trans. and ed. *The Coming of the Friars*. New York: Barnes & Noble, 1975.

Bullough, Vern L. "Medieval Medical and Scientific Views of Women." *Viator* 4 (1973): 485–501.

Bynum, Caroline. *Jesus as Mother: Studies in the Spirituality of the High Middle Ages*. Berkeley: University of California Press, 1982.

Carruthers, Mary J. "Time, Apocalypse, and the Plot of *Piers Plowman*." In Mary J. Carruthers and Elizabeth D. Kirk, eds. *Acts of Interpretation: The Text in Its Contexts, 700–1600: Essays in Honor of E. Talbot Donaldson*. Norman, Okla.: Pilgrim Books, 1982, pp. 175–88.

The Catholic Encyclopedia. New York: Appleton, 1911.

Clopper, Lawrence. "Langland's Trinitarian Analogues as a Key to Meaning and Structure." *M&H*, n.s., 9 (1979): 87–110.

Colledge, E. *The Medieval Mystics in England*. London: Murray, 1962.

Collis, Louise. *The Apprentice Saint*. London: Michael Joseph, 1964.

Conley, John, ed. *The Middle English* Pearl: *Critical Essays*. Notre Dame, Ind.: University of Notre Dame Press, 1970.

Coulton, George G. *From St. Francis to Dante*. 1906. Reprint. Philadelphia: University of Pennsylvania Press, 1972.

Cousins, Ewert H. "The Coincidence of Opposites in the Christology of St. Bonaventure." *EFran* 18 (1963): 15–31.

Cross, Claire. "Great Reasoners in Scripture: The Activities of Women Lollards, 1380–1530." In Derek Baker, ed. *Medieval Women*. Oxford: Basil Blackwell, 1978, pp. 359–80.

Davlin, Mary Clemente. "Kynde Knowyng as a Major Theme in *Piers Plowman* B." *RES*, n.s., 22 (1971): 1–19.

Deanesly, Margaret. "The Gospel Harmony of John de Caulibus or St. Bonaventure." In C. L. Kingsford, ed. *Collectanea Franciscana*. Manchester: Manchester University Press, 1922, 2:10–19.

———. *The Lollard Bible*. Cambridge: Cambridge University Press, 1920.

————. "Vernacular Books in England in the Fourteenth and Fifteenth Centuries." *MLR* 15 (1920): 349–58.

Dickman, Susan. "Margery Kempe and the Continental Tradition of Pious Women." In Marion Glasscoe, ed. *The Medieval Mystical Tradition in England*. Papers Read at Dartington Hall, July 1984. Cambridge: D. S. Brewer, 1984, pp. 150–68.

————. "Margery Kempe and the English Devotional Tradition." In Marion Glasscoe, ed. *The Medieval Mystical Tradition in England*. Papers Read at the Exeter Symposium, July 1980. Exeter: Exeter University Press, 1980, pp. 156–72.

Donaldson, E. Talbot. Piers Plowman: *The C-Text and Its Poet*. New Haven, Conn.: Yale University Press, 1949. 2d ed., 1966.

Dupré, Louis. *The Other Dimension: A Search for the Meaning of Religious Attitudes*. New York: Doubleday, 1972.

Eliade, Mircea. *Patterns in Comparative Religion*. Cleveland, Ohio: World Publishing Co., 1963.

Erikson, Carolly. "The Fourteenth-Century Friars and Their Critics: Part I." *FS* 35 (1975): 107–35.

————. "The Fourteenth-Century Friars and Their Critics: Part II." *FS* 36 (1976): 108–47.

————. *The Medieval Vision*. Oxford: Oxford University Press, 1976.

Evans, W. O. "Charity in *Piers Plowman*." In S. S. Hussey, ed. Piers Plowman: *Critical Approaches*. London: Methuen, 1969, pp. 245–78.

Fleming, John. *An Introduction to the Franciscan Literature of the Middle Ages*. Chicago: Franciscan Herald Press, 1977.

Frank, Robert Worth. Piers Plowman *and the Scheme of Salvation*. New Haven, Conn.: Yale University Press, 1957. Reprint. Hamden, Conn.: Archon Books, 1969.

Fries, Maureen. "Margery Kempe." In Paul Szarmach, ed. *An Introduction to the Medieval Mystics of Europe*. Albany, N.Y.: SUNY Press, 1984, pp. 217–35.

Gilson, Etienne. *The Philosophy of St. Bonaventure*. Paterson, N.J.: St. Anthony Guild Press, 1965.

Gray, Douglas. *Themes and Images in the Medieval Religious Lyric*. Boston: Routledge and Kegan Paul, 1972.

Hamilton, Marie P. "The Meaning of the Middle English *Pearl*." *PMLA* 70 (1955): 805–24.

Harwood, Britton J. "Langland's Kynde Knowyng and the Quest for Christ." *MP* 80 (1983): 242–55.

————. "*Piers Plowman*: Fourteenth Century Skepticism and the Theology of Suffering." *BuR* 19 (1971): 119–36.

Hort, Greta. Piers Plowman *and Contemporary Religious Thought*. 1938. Reprint. New York: Macmillan, 1977.

Howard, Donald. *The Three Temptations: Medieval Man in Search of the World*. Princeton, N.J.: Princeton University Press, 1966.

————. *Writers and Pilgrims: Medieval Pilgrim Narratives and Their Posterity*. Berkeley: University of California Press, 1980.

Huizinga, Johan. *The Waning of the Middle Ages*. Trans. F. Hopman. 1949. Reprint. New York: Doubleday, 1954.

Hussey, S. S., ed. Piers Plowman: *Critical Approaches*. London: Methuen, 1969.

Jeffrey, David L. *The Early English Lyric and Franciscan Spirituality*. Lincoln: University of Nebraska Press, 1975.

Jelenik, Estelle C. *Women's Autobiography*. Bloomington: Indiana University Press, 1980.

Kean, Patricia. "Langland on the Incarnation." *RES*, n.s., 16 (1965): 349–63.

———. The Pearl: *An Interpretation*. London: Routledge and Kegan Paul, 1967.

Kieckhefer, Richard. *Unquiet Souls*. Chicago: University of Chicago Press, 1984.

Kirk, Elizabeth D. *The Dream Thought of* Piers Plowman. New Haven, Conn.: Yale University Press, 1972.

Knowles, David. *The English Mystical Tradition*. New York: Harper & Brothers, 1961.

Kolve, V. A. *Chaucer and the Imagery of Narrative*. Stanford, Calif.: Stanford University Press, 1984.

Latham, R. E. *Revised Medieval Latin Word List*. London: Oxford University Press, 1965.

Lovatt, Roger. "The Imitation of Christ in Late Medieval England." *Transactions of the Royal Historical Society*, 5th ser., vol. 18. London: Butler & Tanner, 1968, pp. 97–122.

Madeleva, Sr. Mary. Pearl: *A Study in Spiritual Dryness*. 1925. Reprint. New York: Phaeton Press, 1968.

Maisonneve, Roland. "Margery Kempe and the Eastern and Western Tradition of the 'Perfect Fool.'" In Marion Glasscoe, ed. *The Medieval Mystical Tradition in England*. Papers Read at Dartington Hall, July, 1982. Exeter: Exeter University Press, 1982, pp. 1–17.

Martz, Louis. *The Poetry of Meditation*. New Haven, Conn.: Yale University Press, 1954.

Mills, David. "The Role of the Dreamer in *Piers Plowman*." In S. S. Hussey, ed. *Piers Plowman: Critical Approaches*. London: Methuen, 1969, pp. 180–212.

Milosh, Joseph E. The Scale [Ladder] of Perfection *and the English Mystical Tradition*. Madison: University of Wisconsin Press, 1966.

Mitchell, A. G. "Lady Meed and the Art of *Piers Plowman*." In Robert Blanch, ed. *Style and Symbolism in* Piers Plowman. Knoxville: University of Tennessee Press, 1969, pp. 174–93.

Moorman, John. *A History of the Franciscan Order*. Oxford: Oxford University Press, 1968.

Morris, Colin. *The Discovery of the Individual*. New York: Harper & Row, 1972.

Nadel, Ira Bruce. *Biography: Fiction, Fact, and Form*. New York: St. Martin's Press, 1984.

Nelson, William. *Fact or Fiction: The Dilemma of the Renaissance Storyteller*. Cambridge, Mass.: Harvard University Press, 1973.

Niermeyer, J. F. *Mediae latinitatus lexicon minus*. Leiden: Brill, 1976.

Nolan, Barbara. *The Gothic Visionary Perspective*. Princeton, N.J.: Princeton University Press, 1977.

Obermann, Heiko A. "The Shape of Late Medieval Thought: The Birthpangs of the Modern Era." In Heiko A. Obermann and Charles Trinkhaus, eds. *The Pursuit of Holiness in Late Medieval and Renaissance Religion*. Leiden: Brill, 1974.

Olney, James. *Metaphors of Self*. Princeton, N.J.: Princeton University Press, 1972.

Oxford Latin Dictionary. Oxford: Oxford University Press, 1982.

Petroff, Elizabeth. *Consolation of the Blessed*. Millerton, N.Y.: Alta Gaia Society, 1979.

Piehler, Paul. *The Visionary Landscape: A Study in Medieval Allegory*. London: Edward Arnold, 1971.

Pourrat, Pierre. *Christian Spirituality in the Middle Ages*. 4 vols. Westminster: New Press, 1953, vol. 1.

Reeves, Marjorie. Introduction. In Bernard McGinn, trans. and ed. *Apocalyptic Spirituality*. New York: Paulist Press, 1979.

Richardson, F. E. "*The Pearl*: A Poem and Its Audience." *Neophil* 46 (1962): 308–16.

Riehle, Wolfgang. *The Middle English Mystics*. Trans. Bernard Standring. London: Routledge and Kegan Paul, 1981.

Salter, Elizabeth. *Nicholas Love's Myrrour of the Blessed Lyf of Jesu Christ*. Vol. 10 of *Analecta Cartusiana*. Ed. James Hogg. Salzburg: Institut für Englische Sprach und Literatur, 1974.

———. "*Piers Plowman* and the Pilgrimage to Truth." In Robert J. Blanch, ed. *Style and Symbolism in* Piers Plowman. Knoxville: University of Tennessee Press, 1969.

Schmidt, A.V. C. "Langland and the Mystical Tradition." In Marion Glasscoe, ed. *The Medieval Mystical Tradition in England*. Papers Read at the Exeter Symposium, July, 1980. Exeter: University of Exeter Press, 1980, pp. 17–38.

Schofield, W. H. "The Nature and Fabric of the *Pearl*." *PMLA* 19 (1904): 154–215.

———. "Symbolism, Allegory, and Autobiography in the *Pearl*." *PMLA* 24 (1909): 585–675.

Spearing, A. C. *The* Gawain *Poet: A Critical Study*. Cambridge: Cambridge University Press, 1970.

———. "Symbolic and Dramatic Development in the *Pearl*." *MP* 60 (1962): 1–12.

Spengemann, William. *The Forms of Autobiography*. New Haven, Conn.: Yale University Press, 1980.

Stallings, M[ary] Jordan. *Meditaciones de Passione Christi olim Sancto Bonaventurae attributae*. Vol. 25 of *The Catholic University Studies in Medieval and Renaissance Latin Language and Literature*. Washington, D.C.: Catholic University Press, 1965.

Tentler, Thomas. *Sin and Confession on the Eve of the Reformation*. Princeton, N.J.: Princeton University Press, 1977.

Thornton, Martin. *Margery Kempe: An Example in the English Pastoral Tradition*. London: SPCK, 1960.

Vasta, Edward. "*Pearl*: Immortal Flowers and the Pearl's Decay." In John Conley, ed. *The Middle English Pearl: Critical Essays*. Notre Dame, Ind.: University of Notre Dame Press, 1970, pp. 185–202.

———, ed. *Interpretations of* Piers Plowman. Notre Dame, Ind.: University of Notre Dame Press, 1968.

Walsh, James, ed. *Pre-Reformation English Spirituality*. New York: Fordham University Press, 1965.

Weintraub, Karl Joachim. *The Value of the Individual: Self and Circumstance in Autobiography*. Chicago: University of Chicago Press, 1978.

Weissman, Hope Phyllis. "Margery Kempe in Jerusalem: *Hysterica Compassio* in the Late Middle Ages." In Mary J. Carruthers and Elizabeth D. Kirk, eds. *Acts of Interpretation: The Text in Its Contexts, 700–1600: Essays on Medieval and Renaissance Literature in Honor of E. Talbot Donaldson*. Norman, Okla.: Pilgrim Books, 1982, pp. 201–17.

Wellek, René. "*The Pearl*: An Interpretation of the Middle English Poem." In Robert J.

Blanch, ed. Sir Gawain *and* Pearl: *Critical Essays*. Bloomington: Indiana University Press, 1966, pp. 37–59.

Wilkins, David. "The Meaning of Space in Fourteenth-Century Tuscan Painting." In David L. Jeffrey, ed. *By Things Seen: Reference and Recognition in Medieval Thought*. Ottawa: Ottawa University Press, 1979, pp. 109–21.

Wittig, Joseph. "*Piers Plowman* B, Passus IX–XII: Elements in the Design of the Inward Journey." *Traditio* 28 (1972): 211–80.

Woolf, Rosemary. *An Introduction to the Religious Lyric in the Middle Ages*. Oxford: Oxford University Press, 1968.

Index